Your Money 2019–20

The beginner's guide to earning, spending, borrowing and saving

Jeannette Lichner

KoganPage

Publisher's note

Every possible effort has been made to ensure that the information contained in this book is accurate at the time of going to press, and the publisher and author cannot accept responsibility for any errors or omissions, however caused. No responsibility for loss or damage occasioned to any person acting, or refraining from action, as a result of the material in this publication can be accepted by the editor, the publisher or the author.

First published in Great Britain and the United States in 2019 by Kogan Page Limited

2nd Floor, 45 Gee Street	122 W 27th St, 10th Floor	4737/23 Ansari Road
London	New York, NY 10001	Daryaganj
EC1V 3RS	USA	New Delhi 110002
United Kingdom		India

www.koganpage.com

ISBNs

Hardback	978 1 78966 015 9
Paperback	978 0 7494 9728 6
Ebook	971 0 7994 9727 9

British Library Cataloguing-in-Publication Data

A CIP record for this book is available from the British Library.

Library of Congress Cataloging-in-Publication Number

2019022462

Typeset by Integra Software Services, Pondicherry
Print production managed by Jellyfish
Printed and bound by CPI Group (UK) Ltd, Croydon, CR0 4YY

CONTENTS

FOREWORD

Despite Brexit, life goes on and we live in an increasingly financially complex world. Finance can seem so daunting, with its own impenetrable language and apparent complexity, that it seems an alien concept. Yet it touches us all and is part of the core infrastructure of our society.

Help is at hand. This book cracks the financial code and unlocks the secrets, revealing that money isn't that complex after all. The book is a jargon buster, shining sunlight on an otherwise opaque world, and explains, in clear, straightforward language, many of the key financial principles. The author dispenses thoughtful advice and tips throughout the book so that the reader can understand how to make the finance sector work for them and make their money go further.

This updated 2019/20 edition covers new products, new rules, new rates, new 'challengers' – be they banks, cards or methods of saving – providing a common-sense view in an ever-changing global economic world.

This new edition has been fully revised to reflect the major changes during the year, including the different rates of income tax between Scotland and the rest of UK, new saving initiatives, new types of payment cards, new rules on dividends and pensions, a new car environment tax, and the rapid growth of contactless payments cards, which now account for well over 50 per cent of all transactions and which didn't exist when this book was first written.

The Chartered Institute for Securities & Investment (CISI) is delighted to continue to support this book and believes that this is one of the best resources for young people, providing real value to the reader. We think it should be essential reading for anyone starting out in the world on their own and having to manage their own money, as it is equally relevant for the 16-year-old who is starting their first job as well as those going on to, or even leaving, university.

I hope you will want to invest time in reading this book, either in bite-sized chunks or all the way through. In return, you will have a much greater understanding of how to make the most of your money.

Simon Culhane, Chartered FCSI
Chief Executive, Chartered Institute
for Securities & Investment
March 2019

PREFACE

This book has been written with everyone who wants to be in control of their money in mind, and is particularly aimed at young people who are between 16 and 25. I wrote this thinking about my own son and daughter and their friends; they were starting to face issues around that age, as they became increasingly financially independent. Ensuring offspring are financially independent is a major parental responsibility, though parents don't necessarily give that goal enough thought.

As I watched them growing up, moving away from home and taking responsibility for longer-term money decisions, I saw them getting frustrated by situations that they didn't see coming. The most common among their crowd, for example, were when they moved in and out of rented places, when they went overdrawn, and when they found themselves short of money at the end of a month or two. I started thinking it would be really useful to have a one-stop place where you could read about the financial stuff you need to know, explained in a way you could easily understand. There is obviously a lot of information available on the internet, and I reference sites in the book... but you can't look up stuff if you don't know what you're looking for!

I figured that with my experience of managing money – sometimes when I had little and sometimes when I had what seemed like a lot – having learned from some money mistakes and having a bit of a skill for explaining things, I would be a good person to try to meet that need, and this is the result.

I hope you enjoy the book as much as I enjoyed writing it. All best wishes for a financially-in-control future!

Jeannette

How to use this book

There are a few ways to read this book: page by page through the entire book; skim the table of contents and read the parts that are relevant to you now; or flip through the book and see what catches your eye. Do whatever works for you – but I do recommend you keep a pen handy to mark up the book or make notes of things you want to do differently, investigate or remember to revisit later.

Whichever you do: **please read the first chapter**. This will help you understand how you think about money, what your values about money are, and how you make money decisions. Studies show that your attitude to money was formed by the time you were seven years old. You may have a healthy attitude that you want to stick with; however, if you *do* want to change anything about it, you need to start that changing *now*. You want to make every big money decision being well aware of why you made that decision. You want to make sure every decision is the one that is right for you, the one where *you* are in control of your money, and never look back at a decision with regret.

ACKNOWLEDGEMENTS

A heartfelt thanks to the many people throughout my years of involvement in improving financial capability in the UK who have given of their time, insights and stories.

A thank you to the Chartered Institute of Securities & Investment, and Simon Culhane in particular, who supported me in editing and distributing earlier books on this same topic.

Thank you to Kogan Page, led by Helen Kogan, for their interest in publishing *Your Money* and for their marketing support to enable a wide distribution, getting the book into the hands of those who would benefit the most. Thank you too to Rebecca Bush, who guided me through the editing and publishing process with infinite patience.

And last but not least, thank you to my family, Andrew, Jessica and Kit, who encourage me in all that I do.

01
You and your money

As we start our money learning journey together, let's explore you and your relationship with money. First, let's increase your awareness about money and the money decisions you make daily. By becoming aware of them, you can evaluate whether they are the right decisions for you. We will then focus on your money values, your attitude to money and what has influenced and will influence those. Again, by being aware, you will be more in control. And that is what we are going to do here. Bring *you* totally in control of all of your money decisions – now and in the future.

Since you're reading this book, chances are you're interested in managing your money, perhaps better than you have historically. Or perhaps you want to learn about the money challenges you will face in the future, and get some facts straight. All good stuff. What you may *not* realize is just how important money management is to your long-term health. Many mental health issues, including stress, have financial worries at their source. And this is the same for all levels of wealth. We develop stress when we're not in control, so no matter how much or how little money you have, stay in control and be confident that you are making the best decisions for you!

Your money situation – become more aware

How many money decisions a day do you think you make? Take some time to think about it and you will find there are more than you thought. Consider not just the decisions around your money, but things that are provided by others that involve money – such as school, holidays, eating out, and food in the fridge.

Maybe you haven't had to think much about money. Maybe you've been financially supported by your parents and they've replenished your money supply whenever you asked them to. Or maybe you've thought a lot about it.

Perhaps you've worked throughout the school year or holidays, earned all your own spending money, saved up for university or to buy something special. Or perhaps your parents did give you money and you've had to manage that money really carefully to get through each month. Your financial situation may be any of those and anything in between.

Whatever your situation, now is a good time to start paying more attention to your money, giving more thought to the choices you make, consciously or otherwise, and evaluating whether you want to make changes to what you are currently doing.

One decision at a time; and sometimes they are hard

If you consider your typical day, what money decisions do you make and what alternative choices could you make? In the box are a few thoughts which give you an idea of what I mean.

EXERCISE Try this – daily money decisions

Make a list for your average day and note down everything you typically do, and what decisions you make about money. Keep in mind that some of the decisions have been made in the past, even what type of shampoo you use or what school you go to:

- Get up, shower (what soap? shampoo?), have breakfast (at home? Buy it on the go?)

- Meet a friend at a coffee shop, have a takeaway coffee. (Can you bring your own or meet elsewhere?)

- Go to classes or work. (Walk, cycle, take the bus, take the tube, drive?)

- After classes/work (drive, walk?) to the gym (do you have a good deal?) and then to visit a friend. (Spend anything there?)

- Settle down to work or study. (Heating on or off? Lights on or off in rooms you passed through on your way to your desk?)

- Meet up with friends for dinner (in halls, at the pub, at home?) and plan a holiday. (Is it really what you want to do? How will you pay for it? What will you have to give up in order to pay for it?)

What did you find? Did you come up with anything surprising? Maybe the total number of money decisions you made surprised you. Or maybe the number of money decisions you made in advance, like your mobile phone contract and your internet access package, was surprising. Maybe you found that you spend much more money in one day, without thinking about it, than you expected. Or maybe you spend less than you expected? You may find it a fun challenge to see how low you can get your one-day number – or how high?

You don't need to think long and hard about every money decision; for small amounts, just get on with it. What you want to do is pay more attention and invest time in evaluating options when you are spending a big chunk of money or committing to something for a long period of time. But – and this is a big but – for most of us, the surprise comes from small-ish amounts we spend regularly. The one people raise with me most often is buying coffee every day: this can result in a total spend of around £700 per year. There is nothing wrong with that, if it's what you want to spend your money on, but you want to make sure you are making a conscious decision. Similarly for eating lunch out; several people have expressed their surprise at the total amount they spent on this. Again, totally fine – just check yourself to make sure you are doing what you want, consciously, not purely out of habit.

How often, if ever, do you and your friends have differing views about doing something because of the money involved? Do you always agree on spending for things like phones, going to the pub, going to sports matches or concerts, shopping for clothes or going out to eat? It would be surprising if you always did! Some of your friends, or you, may 'have to have' the latest and greatest of whatever (phone, clothes, sports equipment) and some may not. Some may like to hold onto their money and others may spend it without thinking. Some may love to 'flash their cash' and others may be downright miserly. Some of your friends may have what seems like lots of money available to them and others may seem to have little. Have you ever felt uncomfortable for yourself or for a friend because of something to do with money? How did you handle it? How would you handle it next time?

Sometimes it is hard to decide what to do when you face a money decision. A few examples: Should you work all weekend rather than do something with your friends? Should you spend your money on that new phone or going to a concert? Can you recall having a particularly difficult time making a money decision or helping a friend make one? The debate always seems to end up being around whether something is 'worth it' or not. But how do you figure out if something *is* 'worth it' until 'it' is done? Those decisions can be particularly hard if the sums are relatively large, because each of you may be in a different financial situation. Spending £20, if it is all the money you will have for the next week, is a different proposition from when it is all the money you will have for the next month. So, if you and your friends are in different money places, it's totally natural for you to have different views and judgements about what to do with your money. Being aware that those differences exist is useful to avoid falling out about a decision to do or buy something.

As you go about your daily routine, think about the money decisions you make and what may be influencing you. And be in tune with your friends to explore how they make their decisions and what may be influencing them.

Early money memories shape our values

Studies show that our values about money are formed by the time we are seven years old. I can't remember being seven, but I can totally see that my upbringing impacted my view about money – for better or worse! Think back to your early experiences of money and think about how your view has evolved through the life experiences that have shaped your current perspective.

Here are a few questions that may help prompt you as you reflect:

- Do you remember constantly wanting things you saw advertised on TV?
- What did your parents say when you asked them to get you the same stuff that kids in your class had?
- Do you remember being totally unaware about money? (I was told some lovely stories by parents about their young children marking up Argos and Toys 'R' Us catalogues to show everything they wanted.)
- The first time you had your own money to spend, what was the first big spending decision you made?
- When did you start getting pocket money or an allowance?
- When you started earning your own money, what did it feel like? What did you do with it?

Chances are there are a few events that have had a big impact on you and stick with you today. There will be others that you have let go of, or perhaps moved in the totally opposite direction. Keep in mind that nothing is right or wrong here; you're just trying to understand how you make decisions or react to money questions.

Your past influences your attitude to money today

Every adult I know can recall what their family's financial situation was like when they were growing up, and the impact that their upbringing had on their values and life. When I collected people's stories, which I did from a wide range of backgrounds, the same topics kept coming up as major shapers of current money attitudes. I have posed them as questions to help you with some self-reflection:

- Was your family well off, middling, or struggling financially? What was your family's situation compared with families around you? When did you become aware of any differences? How did they make you feel?

- Did you grow up in a one-parent household? Or with both parents? With other family members?

- What family members did you see going to work on a regular, frequent or infrequent basis? Was your family partially or fully reliant on government benefits?

- What financial choices did your parents, or other adults responsible for you, make? What did they choose to spend money on, if they were able to make choices? What was considered a 'luxury' in your home?

- What was the view on education? Holidays? Eating out? Owning a home?

- How were possessions treated? Valued and protected? Disposable?

- What was used to pay for things – cash or credit cards? Were you aware of debts – growing credit card balances, overdrafts or loans?

- Were there open discussions about money – earning, spending and saving it? What were they like?

Your sense of financial independence and responsibility will also have been influenced by your home life. The questions below relate to your attitude emerging from that:

- Did your parents give you spending money? How old were you when you started to receive it?

- Did you have to work for that money by doing things around your home?

- When did you start earning your own money?

- How financially independent do you think you are now?

Lots of things to think about, I know! I am asking you to do this because change only happens through self-awareness, so even if this is stressful or hard work, I encourage you to spend time thinking about this.

> 'My parents didn't have a lot of money in a town that was upper middle class, so while everyone else was driving around in nice cars, our driveway was filled with tyres and spares... I was, like, this is not how I want to live.'
>
> Comedian and chat show host Chelsea Handler on what lies behind her drive for success. *The Mail on Sunday*

Today's influences on your attitude to money

While we parents like to think we continue to influence our sons and daughters, there are other influences that are stronger than ours as our sons and daughters grow up. They include the following.

Your friends

You, like most people, probably have a desire to be part of a group, to 'fit in' with the crowd you spend time with. It isn't therefore surprising that the lifestyles your friends lead, their families' financial situations and how they make money decisions are going to impact you.

When I was writing this book, many people shared stories about feeling awkward because they couldn't buy or do things that their friends could. I noticed that people only talked about having less than others, never about being the one 'with the most'. (There is something about human nature there that is not so good.)

You and your friends may also have differing views about earning money. Some of your friends may work, or may have worked, during school terms and/or holidays, and some may not have. Some of your friends may feel they have to work really hard to earn money and some may have a more casual approach to work. It is useful to notice those differing attitudes, consider what impact they are having on you and make sure you are happy with the attitude *you* have.

Your friends' money decisions are influenced by their pasts, but you'll find you can't predict the future from the past. You may notice that some friends who grew up surrounded by money are very careful with it to the point of being a bit 'tight', and some friends who had very little money growing up are now 'carefree' (even careless) with their money. And vice versa, and every possibility in between.

Hobbies and interests

The types of activities you get involved with will impact your perspective on money. For example, if you get involved in expensive things, you will probably need to do some earning and saving. If your interests are low-cost, you may not need to. Some hobbies and interests, such as cycling or serious photography, require big upfront investments. Some are expensive on the day, like going to watch sports matches or concerts. On the other hand, some sports like running and walking are nearly free. Socializing definitely can be expensive and that does count as a hobby!

College or university

If you go to college or university you will meet, or will have met, people from a wide range of financial backgrounds. You are likely to meet people who are financially better off and worse off than you. You may also get glimpses into the financial values of your friends' families.

Avoid making assumptions about people based on what you see, as you will be working with limited information. For example, you might assume that a friend who lives in a huge house is wealthy, and if they live in a small house they aren't. Who knows what choices that family has made? Some people choose to invest all their money in their house and have little excess cash – they are property rich/cash poor. And sometimes people put up a façade that all is financially fine when it isn't: they are heavily in debt. So avoid gauging an individual or family financial situation from how you see people spending their money. Take the opportunity to observe the money values and attitudes of the wide range of people you meet during this phase of your life and think about what influence you want them to have on *your* attitude.

Work colleagues

Whether you work part-time or full-time, chances are this group is one that you may want to 'fit in with'. If you're working full-time, you're likely to spend more time with your colleagues than with anyone else in your life. Be aware of the variety of views about money that you come across and once again observe the range of perspectives and financial situations of your colleagues.

It's very easy to fall into the same spending patterns as those you work with and inadvertently get carried along with the crowd. It can be really hard to say 'no thanks, I want to save my money' when everyone is going out after work. It is also hard to say 'no' when the group starts planning a weekend away, or when everyone decides to go watch a big rugby match. You may think it would be a real black mark if you don't go along with the crowd. People I spoke with all thought that would be the case for them. But, when I asked them how they would react if someone turned down a suggestion of theirs, they said it would be fine. So don't assume you will be harshly judged for opting out of something you choose not to do.

Alcohol and drugs

When I collected stories about losing or wasting money, I frequently heard stories that involved an element of alcohol or other drugs. These included: 'losing' money during nights out; forgetting to take money out of the cash machine that had been withdrawn; and 'wasting' money on long taxi rides home. Your decisions about drink and drugs are yours, but do be aware that if you are partaking, it's easy to lose track of what you're doing with your money. I heard a few good ideas to help minimize the risk of wastage (no pun intended). The most frequent suggestion was this: when you go out for an evening, only take the amount of money you really want to spend and don't take your debit or credit card with you. Since you don't want to have to make a dangerous journey home because you have no money, stick with your friends and have one of you stay sober enough to make sure everyone gets home safely.

Contrasting money decisions

Here are a few stories I heard when I did my research that show just how different money decisions can be, focusing on the generation gap between parents and their children:

- 'Wow, it costs me £2 to have a shirt laundered when I drop it at the shop on my way to work.' The parent pointed out that there was a cheaper place around the corner. One parent was surprised that laundry was being sent out at all.

- 'How much do these young women spend on manicures, pedicures and haircutting?' A few parents expressed surprise at the money spent on grooming these days. They wondered why people didn't think about doing these things themselves or just skipping them.

- 'I spend about £5 a day on lunch.' The cost of lunch was a frequently mentioned money concern. Some people are good at scouting out meal deals at shops, using coupons or finding two-for-one restaurant deals. Relatively few people I met considered making their own lunches, which the previous generation frequently did.

- 'Young people spend much more on eating out than we did at their age.' Parents said this often. The cost of eating out is now less relative to salaries than it was for the previous generation and, therefore, it isn't perceived as the luxury it once was. That's not the case for everyone, though! Food money is the area where you can probably influence your spending the most, by choosing proactively between eating out, eating prepared meals in, and cooking with raw ingredients. A few people explained they had limited choices because they didn't know how to cook – which is definitely fixable! Check out the new businesses where all of the cooking ingredients needed to create a meal are delivered to your home – names such as 'Hello Fresh', 'Mindful Chef', 'Simply Cook' and 'Gousto' are ones you may have seen. Remember that you can also save money by ordering food to be delivered or by buying a takeaway, meaning that you save the high cost of drinks in restaurants.

Money does not make you happy

One value that you don't want to creep into your attitude is the idea that if you have lots of money you will be happy. A fundamental truth that has been proven time and again is that, while money can buy most things, it does not buy happiness. True, money (or the lack of it) can *impact* happiness: Abraham Maslow, a renowned psychologist, defined a hierarchy of needs that humans seek to meet. These needs are, in priority order, having food and water, shelter and safety, love and belonging, and self-esteem. Obviously, food, water, shelter and safety (at least) can all be affected by money. There are people who do not have their fundamental needs met – childhood hunger and poverty, for example, are not things reserved for developing countries; we have them here in the UK. The levels of homelessness and people using foodbanks are shocking and increasing, so don't be complacent.

Once basic needs are met, though, what role does money provide in motivating us and enhancing our happiness? Frederick Herzberg, the eminent psychologist, asserts: 'The powerful motivator in our lives isn't money; it's the opportunity to learn, grow in responsibilities, contribute to others and be recognized for achievements.' Additional studies show that it is the recognition of our achievements and contributions that matter most to us. We will explore this in Chapter 3, but for now, just hold the thought that you create your own happiness – it comes from within you, not from the pounds in your bank account or the stuff you own.

Your money personality

Now that you have explored the past and present influences on your attitude to money, take a moment or two to consolidate your thinking about what your views really are. What money situations have you felt uncomfortable with? Or noticed others feeling uncomfortable with? How would you describe your financial character? What do you value and are willing to work or save for? How do you like to spend your money? How do you decide what is 'worth it' or not? How do you feel about working and earning money?

EXERCISE Try this – what kind of money personality are you?

When it comes to spending money, people tend to fall into one of four categories. Work through the questions that follow, to see which one best describes you:

1 When you earn or receive money, are you most likely to:

   A Spend it as soon as you see something you like?

   B Put it into your bank current account as you are likely to spend it soon?

   C Put it directly into a savings account to fund something expensive you are saving for?

2 When your phone bill arrives at the end of the month, your reaction is likely to be:

   A Shocked beyond words and thinking, 'How did I spend so much?'

   B Pleased that you are a bit over or under your contract.

   C Pleased that you are well under your contract again this month and thinking about calling the provider to renegotiate your contract.

3 You and your friends are planning a trip together and it is turning into a bigger, more expensive one than you expected and can afford. You will:

   A Go along with the plans as you don't want to miss out – you'll figure the money out later.

   B Get the group talking about other options to get to a final plan that is affordable for everyone.

   C Let the plans proceed but decide not to go along on the trip, unless you are going to have time to save up for it.

4 How often do you put money in your savings account:

   A Never. You don't have a savings account.

   B Occasionally.

   C All the time. Every time you have excess cash you put it away to avoid the temptation to spend it.

5 How often do you use your overdraft, go overdrawn, or need to borrow money from somewhere?

   A Most months.

   B Very rarely, maybe once a year.

   C Never. You never get even close to that situation.

- Mostly As: you are a spender and you may find that your money seems to just disappear.

- Mostly Bs: you are a fairly balanced saver/spender, confident about what you do and don't want to spend your money on and how much you want to have in savings.

- Mostly Cs: you fall into the saver category and are very careful about how you spend your money, preferring to miss out on something if you don't have the money for it. Do be careful not to turn into a miser (the fourth stereotype) though. You can lose friends by not paying your fair share of things, or not doing even low-cost things, because of money.

Chances are you had a mixture of responses to the questions. If you think more broadly about your own life, you will see that you will fall into a different category depending on the situation. Now that you have increased your awareness of money decisions and your underlying knowledge, you will be more likely to make the right decisions for you every time.

My reflections on money

While I was writing this book, I thought a lot about my own attitude to money; the mistakes I had made, what I had learned and the smart decisions I had made. I also thought about what makes each of us feel stressed about money, irrespective of our financial situation.

When I reflected on myself and my observation of others, it's clear to me that financial stress doesn't come from how much money you do or don't have. The stress comes from feeling out of control or having no discipline about your financial situation. My three simple concepts to help you to live less stressful lives moneywise are:

- Control your destiny – be in charge of your own decisions, rather than being overly influenced by others. Have enough confidence in yourself and respect for your values to stick to your convictions.

- Make decisions you are likely to like with hindsight – this is easier said than done! Avoid the 'wish I hadn't, what a waste of money, why did I buy those?' regrets. Ensure you give yourself time when you are making an important decision – 'sleep on it'.

- Think about what is driving your decision – what is the motivation for it? Are you making the decision based on what is right for you or someone else? Is it a short-term desire that may not really matter tomorrow? Is it about being accepted by others? Is it a decision that sits comfortably with you and your money values?

Closing thoughts

By now, you will be warmed up to the topic of money and will have given some thought to your personal history and your current views about it. You will also understand the impact that your upbringing and current situation have on your attitude to money.

> **TIP**
>
> Great monetary successes frequently come from financially adverse circumstances, humble beginnings and unusual career paths. Think of J K Rowling, who wrote *Harry Potter* while on benefits. Think of Jamie Oliver, the famous chef. Think of David and Victoria Beckham, who have multifaceted careers that they built from nothing. Don't let your financial past dictate your financial future.

It makes sense, on many levels, to consider money implications when making decisions about today and your future. Many adults told me that 'young adults aren't interested in the long term' but that's not what I found when I talked with people. They expressed concerns about deciding whether or not to go to university, not knowing what options were available for vocational training, whether they would find a job, whether or not they would ever be able to buy a home, and whether and how they would ever be able to save any money. These are real, practical concerns.

What I heard very clearly was a desire to learn *in advance* of making mistakes. Everyone was interested in understanding why they spend money the way they do, what influences their decisions and how they can manage whatever money they have better and smarter. They also asked me about saving money and asked for help to do that.

By thinking about *how* you make your decisions about earning, spending, saving and borrowing money, you will be able to evaluate whether you want to make any changes to your approach. The information in this book will give you the technical know-how to make specific decisions, armed with facts. Ultimately, the goal is for you to spend your money the way *you choose to* – today and in the future.

Everyone is waking up to the fact that being in control of whatever amount of money you have is good for you and your mental health. That control reduces stress, which is the root cause of many illnesses, including mental illnesses. There are many tools beyond this book to help you learn more about money. If you search the web for 'money management podcasts' or 'money podcasts', several will appear. Two of my favourites are *Meaningful Money* by Pete Matthew and *The Financial Wellbeing Podcast*.

I hope you see yourself and your money more clearly, and make great decisions *for you* going forward!

02
The bigger picture

In this chapter we are going to go BIG! We're going to put your decisions about money into the greater context, recognizing that your goal is to keep focused on making the right financial decisions for *you*, always. We will consider two things here that will impact your finances. The first is the economic and political environment and the second is the three fundamental economic principles that *always* hold true.

The economy, politics and you

As we're going about our day-to-day business, it's possible to ignore the economic and political machinations going on around us, though it's pretty hard to ignore them when you think about your finances. The reason is that uncertainty in the world creates uncertainty for your finances; perhaps not in the short term (although the Brexit outcome may), but definitely in the longer term.

The UK government, like each of us, is trying to keep its spending and borrowing in check. But how do they do that when there are factions (eg politicians, unions, citizens) with such different views? What will happen with the National Health Service where, despite huge spending, we are reaching a crisis? Similarly, the education system is creaking. What will happen to the Universal Credit programme? What about other benefits? What will happen with Brexit? And perhaps most relevant to many of you, what is going to happen when interest rates go up, as they most likely will? The level of personal borrowing in the UK is now higher than before the 2008 financial crisis, which means we may be heading towards another big financial crisis.

The answers to these and more questions are uncertain, and while it can feel like we are in particularly wild times, you're always going to be impacted by decisions that are outside of your control. You need to plan for things that may change and influence your finances and make your decisions based on your views. The main areas you will be impacted by are: taxes you will have to pay; the rate of inflation that impacts the cost of things you want to buy and is also likely to impact your pay; the interest rate you are charged for borrowing money; the interest you earn from putting money on deposit in a bank account; and the earnings you make on investments in the stock market, property and other assets.

The message here is that you need to keep aware of what's happening in the politics and economies of the UK and other countries.

The impact of UK politics on you

The UK political and economic situation directly impacts your money situation in a few tangible ways that I want to highlight.

UK Budget Day

Each autumn, the Chancellor of the Exchequer sets out to Parliament a report on the state of the economy, any proposed changes to the tax system, and an annual budget for the country. What's communicated that day impacts all of us, and it does so immediately. The Chancellor declares what government income and what government spending will go up and down. There will be quite a bit of speculation in the press in the run-up to Budget Day, so the declarations are usually not a total surprise.

Key areas that will impact you that are frequently adjusted include: personal allowance level (how much money you can earn before having to pay income tax); the amount of tax on wine, beer, cider and spirits; income tax rates; the tax on petrol; and lots of other things. Make it a point to read the papers after the next Budget Day to see a full list and the economic debate that follows.

Which party is in charge of running the UK?

Each political party (Conservative, Labour, Scottish National Party (SNP), Liberal Democrat and UK Independence Party (UKIP)) has different views about how to manage the country's economy. Therefore, you'll be directly affected by which party is in power. The tools they have at their disposal to manage the country's finances include tax rates, interest rates and inflation rates (though they say the Bank of England controls these last two) on the income side. They have differing approaches to managing the spending side as well, which is managed via government budgets by department. In my view, politicians have overspent in the United States, the UK, across the EU and elsewhere for way too long.

The press

As the impact of digital/social media has increased, things in politics and the economy happen faster than before. Make sure you listen to a variety of perspectives, reading differing views from newspapers and magazines, listening to several news channels and listening to broadcasts to get a broad and balanced view on financial matters. Most newspapers have pretty good money sections on weekends that give investment ideas, mortgage rates and other money- and economy-related stories. The internet is a great resource for learning as well – search on any big topic and you will find plenty to learn from.

Taxes

The rates for income tax, capital gains tax, value added tax, petrol tax and other taxes are all set by the government and they all impact you!

Interest rates

The Head of the Bank of England is called the Governor and chairs the Monetary Policy Committee (MPC), which sets the base rate of interest in the UK. The decisions the MPC makes are important to you, because if you are borrowing or lending money, the rate charged/paid will be based on that rate. Since the 2008 global financial crisis, interest rates in the UK have been very low. In August 2018 they increased from 0.25 per cent to 0.75 per cent, the first time the base rate had risen above 0.5 per cent since March 2009. Before the financial crisis the base rate was over 5.5 per cent, and I remember a time when the interest rate on my mortgage was 13 per cent!

The rate of inflation

The Bank of England also tries to manage the rate of inflation. This is the rate at which the overall cost of living, meaning the cost of buying the same things now as you did before, is increasing. You will often see the term 'inflation rate' referred to in the press. It has hovered around 2 per cent for the past few years, but this may change, probably increasing. This is because there are so many uncertainties, including whether people will be buying more or less than in the past; the availability of credit, which enables people to buy things; and the rate of unemployment, which is an indicator of how many people will have money to buy things.

Interesting percentage dynamics

- If the rate of interest you are earning on your money on deposit in a bank is less than the rate of inflation, you are losing purchasing power by keeping money in the bank rather than spending it or investing it somewhere else where you earn a higher return.

- If your earnings (ie salary) are not increasing at least as fast as the rate of inflation, you are losing purchasing power.

We are living in weird economic times, but there have been lots of 'weird economic times' in the past. In the past 25 years I have seen the following:

- One British pound worth one US dollar; one British pound worth two US dollars.

- Mortgage interest rates at 15 per cent; mortgage interest rates at 3 per cent; and mortgage interest rates at 0 per cent for some borrowers.

- Money on deposit in a simple bank savings account earning 6 per cent interest; money on deposit earning no interest.

- The top rate of income tax on earned income at 60 per cent and 98 per cent on unearned income (interest and dividends); a top rate of tax on earned income at 40 per cent.

- The rate of inflation at 6 per cent a year in the UK and more than 100 per cent a week in South Africa.

- Lots of planning was needed to get money out of a bank: no money machines, no chip and PIN on credit cards (that system came in around 2007), banks were only open between 9 am and 5 pm, credit cards were hardly used and cheques were written for just about everything. And now, cash machines are available everywhere as well as contactless cards where you don't need a PIN or anything to pay for items up to a limited amount (£30 for the time being).

The three fundamental economic principles

These three principles hold true for money matters and other matters, which means you want to think about them each time you make a financial decision (particularly those with long-term consequences).

The risk/reward trade-off

Simply stated, the *more* risk you take, the *more* you should expect to be rewarded for it. By the same token, the *less* risk you take, the *less* you should expect to be rewarded for it. It's a notion you can use in all aspects of life, and it is a principle that helps make sense of many things in life, as you will read later.

This means that if someone is considering giving you a loan and you look like a high-risk borrower, that lender will expect to be paid more than if you were considered to be a lower-risk borrower. You'll read about how banks and other lenders decide how risky you are. You'll also read about what you can do with your excess cash and how to determine how risky you want to be with that money.

Here are a few other examples of how the risk/reward trade-off works:

- Careers – if you take a safe, reliable, easy job, you may earn a steady salary but you are unlikely to make a huge amount of money. If you try to set up your own business, the risk to you is much higher. You may fail or you may get it right and make millions. There has been plenty written about Richard Branson – it is no surprise that one of his teachers told him he would end up either in jail or very wealthy.

- Earning interest – here is an example to bring this to life. In the run-up to the financial crisis, interest rates in the UK were falling and people with cash were frustrated because they earned so little interest on money they had in their bank. Along came Icesave, from Iceland, offering interest rates way above the others. So individuals, businesses, local authorities and charities I know invested their money there. People didn't give much thought as to why the interest rate was higher, or what would happen if Icesave had problems (the UK government provides guarantees on the first £85,000 you hold at a UK bank). When Icesave went bankrupt, people lost their money. They took all that risk to benefit from a 3.5 per cent interest rate rather than 1.5 per cent and the risk became a reality. Happily for the investors, the UK government bailed them out in the end.

- Current interest rates – why do banks currently give you so little interest if you have funds on deposit with them? Quite simply, the Bank of England base rate is low and the banks don't need to reward you for the risk of leaving deposits with them, as they're unlikely to fail. You will learn in Chapter 6 on savings that banks don't pay you anything for money kept in a current account; they pay you a *bit* for money kept in a savings account that you can access at any time; and they pay you a *bit* more if you agree to leave your money with the bank for a longer, agreed period of time. The longer the period, the greater the relative amount they need to pay you, because the risk of you needing it and not being able to get to it is a risk that you are bearing.

- Asking people out – the trade-off works here too. Every time you ask someone out, you are taking the risk that you may be rejected. But if you don't ask, there is zero chance of going out at all.

Supply and demand

This concept is fundamental to setting the price of goods and services. It considers the relationship between people wanting to buy something (demand) and people providing it (supply). In practical terms, and relative to the price of something today:

- If there is a large supply of something and little demand, the price of that something will go down.

- If there is a limited supply of something and lots of demand, the price of that something will go up.

- If the supply and demand for something are pretty much in balance, the price of that something will remain as it is.

Manufacturers of products can control the pricing of their 'something' by controlling the supply. They can influence demand – to an extent – by having a great product that everyone likes, but then copycats appear, which rebalances supply and demand. Think about petrol and the changing prices you see advertised on station forecourts – they go up each time we think the Middle East may reduce oil production. Think also about the price of tickets for football matches that is influenced by how well the team is performing during the season.

On the flip side, think of areas where you have seen prices decrease. The first one that comes to mind for me is technology – mobile phones, laptops and tablets. Each new model starts off expensive and then decreases – sometimes quickly.

This concept will impact your earnings as well as your spending. If you follow a job or career path that *anyone* can do, the pay is likely to be relatively low. If, on the other hand, you are in a job that few people are in, but for which huge demand develops, your pay is likely to increase. Of course, it is hard to predict what jobs/careers will be in demand, so that is not a good basis on which to make a job/career decision, but it is useful to understand that this principle is at work. The concept also applies to you and your reputation at work. If you are known for being great at what you do, employers will want you to work for them and will be willing to pay extra to get you.

The time value of money

This concept works equally but opposite on earning and spending money:

- Getting money now is better than getting money later. Why? Because you can earn interest on that money. And if someone pays you money later, you expect to get paid for waiting for your money in the form of interest.

- Paying money later is better than paying money now. Why? Because you can earn interest on that money until you have to pay it.

Keep a close eye on the economic and political scene in the UK, Europe and beyond, as it will impact your financial situation in the short and long term. If you understand that, and keep the three economic principles in mind as you work to make sense of the world of money, you'll be well positioned to make good decisions!

03
Earning money

This chapter will help you think about your views on earning money, your earning aspirations, and the education and work experience decisions that you are making now that may impact your long-term earnings.

Your changing perspective

When you were young, most of your financial needs were probably met by your parent(s) and they may have discussed what they were earning or other financial things around you. As your full-time education career ends, or ended, you will obviously have to earn money. The question is how much you need – which is driven by how much you spend.

Ninety-nine per cent of students I surveyed indicated that they expected to support themselves immediately or soon after leaving education. Many hoped to go to university, which has money-spending, as well as earnings aspiration, implications. (If university is an important topic for you right now, turn to Chapter 10.) Only 1 per cent of students I surveyed said they planned to live on government benefits. That's good news – self-sufficiency is positive! The big question is *how* to earn money; and the choices are greater than ever, though I realize it may not feel like that.

Did you know?

The unemployment rate is less than 4 per cent right now, which is really low, so if you're looking for a job, keep the faith – you *will* find one. But the rate varies around the country.

Why work?

Throughout this book, my goal is to present things objectively… but here, I'm afraid I *can't*. I am a *big* believer in work – and the sooner the better! Just getting out of the house to do anything, and get paid, is good for anyone. Of course, there are reasons why some people can't work, but for those who can, it tends to make them feel more fulfilled.

The government has been looking hard at the benefits system and has figured out that for some people on benefits, they lose so much money by working that *not* working makes more financial sense. While changes are being introduced, they have not worked to plan. While there *are* issues, the intention to reduce benefits except for those who really need them is expected to become a reality in the near term.

There are four main reasons why you will benefit from working, whatever the job:

- **Boosts your self-esteem** – there's something very satisfying about going to work, doing a good job and getting paid for it. The praise for a job well done, even if just a 'thank you for coming in', is good for your morale and self-confidence. Most people find that being part of a team is fun. And, just as working boosts your self-esteem, *not* working can drain self-esteem.

- **One job leads to others** – we all think that we are supposed to love our job from the outset. But for most people, particularly in the early stages of careers, that may not be the case. Very few people get the right job, in the right company, with the right people, first time around. Data shows that 60 per cent of entry-level job holders change companies within one year of starting their job. All you're looking for in your first job is an environment you like and the opportunity to do things you're good at. Those two things increase the chances of your doing well at your job; and one job leads to another, and another. What's most important is doing each job as if it were the most fascinating ever… that's what gets you the next job!

- **Social interaction** – human beings are social creatures. Even the most introverted people I know gain pleasure from being in the company of others. Managers and supervisors at work aim to create a sense of community and team, which you get to be a part of when you're at work. That sense of belonging is likely to be important to you to some degree, as we all like to be part of something bigger than ourselves. I've had a few terrible jobs, but I always liked hanging out with the people I worked with.

- **Earning money** – I have yet to meet anyone who doesn't get satisfaction from getting paid. Seeing the fruits of your labour in cash or transferred into your bank account feels pretty good. The earnings alone won't sustain your enthusiasm for a job that doesn't have anything else you like about it, but for most people, being paid helps get through even the most tedious of jobs.

Moving from education to work

The transition from education into work can be a huge motivational and emotional challenge. Schools and universities are supposed to help, but the level of support provided is inconsistent based on anecdotes I hear. The government is funding initiatives to assist people in preparing for interviews and jobs, which will also help increase their self-confidence. If you've recently been applying for jobs and been turned down repeatedly, you'll have a glimpse into how a lifetime of job application rejection could impact a person's morale. That experience would make it pretty hard to get motivated to start applying again. And, if you were in a family where you didn't see people going to work, it would be even harder and scarier to get going.

I can understand why young people can feel discouraged when they enter the job market. The recruitment process has become quite impersonal – you submit an application and hear nothing back. And facing repeated rejection because 'you don't have experience' is irritating. By following a few basic processes described here and sticking with it, I know you will find a job. I say that because I've coached many young people who had lost their confidence – and then *did* find a job. You're just looking for ONE job out there!

It really helps get you hired if you have been working at something, from the age you were able to. It doesn't matter what the job is; just showing that you can be relied upon to turn up for work when you are supposed to, and do a good job at whatever the job is, is a positive start. That's another plea to do work – of any sort! – before you move into full-time employment.

What are your earning goals and dreams?

Earlier in this book, we explored influences on your attitudes towards money. These influences will impact your earnings aspirations, but *how* they do it is unpredictable. For example, some people I know who had very little money growing up have been driven to earn a lot of money, and some are the opposite. On the flip side, some people I know who had lots of money growing up can't be bothered to work as they know they'll always be provided for, and some are totally driven to earn money, sometimes trying to prove they can be financially better off than their parents. There are also some people from both types of backgrounds who drop out to live fairly bohemian lifestyles, rejecting money and wealth of any sort. For the most part, though, people I've met in all aspects of my life are just trying to lead financially comfortable and contented lives.

This is a good time in your life to think about what lifestyle you want, as the decisions you make now, about your education, early jobs and longer-term career, will impact your future. How would you describe your financial aspirations or goals? Here are the most common responses I received when I did a survey, which show the diversity of views:

- 'To earn good money.' 'To be able to work only two jobs to make ends meet.' 'To earn a comfortable living.'
- 'To be better off than my parents.' 'To have the same lifestyle as my parents.'
- 'To be able to send my kids to good schools.' 'To be able to send my kids to university.'
- 'To own an Aston Martin DB9.' 'To own a car.'
- 'To have two nice holidays a year.' 'To travel loads.' 'To see the world.'

What are your financial dreams now? How do you think they might change over time? Things will change for you in the coming years that will impact your earnings and spending. Like what? Decisions about further education, a job, a job change, a career change, moving to another country, getting married, having children and so on. Who knows what is just around the corner?

Thinking about your future

Did you know?

- The average household income in the UK with two adults working is £40,000. For single households in the UK, the average is £16,000; but that belies a high of £35,000 in London and a low of £11,000 in Nottingham.

- People earning £50,000 have consistently tested as 'the happiest' in the UK.

- One per cent of people in the UK earn more than £150,000 per year.

If I collected reactions from you and other readers to the statistics in the box, I would get a range. Some people think £40,000 and £35,000 are big numbers and others think they are small. The same goes for the £50,000. And what about the 1 per cent statistic? These three figures are useful markers for you to use as you set your lifestyle and earnings expectations. Remember that the 99.9 per cent of us in the real world (not 'instant' celebrities or zillionaires) will have to earn our money the hard way, by turning up for work every day. So find something you like doing enough to do a lot of it. I am an avid reader of people's life stories, and one thing that always strikes me is that people who are really financially successful are always passionate about what they do.

You may be tempted to skip the next section, wondering why you should spend time now on long-term stuff when you're already at a busy time of life. Well, there are two simple reasons. One – you'll find that life is *always* busy, and you can fill your days with all sorts of activities; you will only find those things that will lead you to a more fulfilling life if you make space in your life to find them. Two – in moments of quiet, you will have the greatest insights into what you want to do with your life, so get your subconscious working on these big issues when you are busy doing other things.

Take time to think about:

- What do you want from your life? What do you want to achieve professionally? Personally? What's important for you to have done by the time you are 30? 40?

- How much time do you plan to dedicate to work? What does managing a work/life balance mean to you? If you have a family, will that influence your commitment to your career or the hours you will be willing to dedicate to it? What interests do you want to have time to pursue?

- Try to picture what your life will be like in five or ten years. What will it cost you to 'get by'? What extra money will you need for your life's pleasures? Do you hope to raise a family? Where do you plan to live? All of these questions and more (I won't list them, as you know what yours are) will influence what you will aim to earn.

- Can you quantify these things? What are your numbers? What is your earnings target for next year? Five years from now? Your lifetime? What will you be willing to sacrifice to achieve those aims? What will you gain?

Working through these questions throughout your life, as you find yourself in the day-to-day work world or when you are making career decisions, will help keep you grounded on what you want from your life.

Did you know?

There are websites where you can offer and trade your freelance skills and services, such as fivesquids.com, upwork.com, taskrabbit.co.uk and fiverr.co.uk.

It was only in my 40s that I learned the power of expressing my own goals in a positive way. Up until then, my personal goal was 'to not be poor'... which is not a very useful goal. When would I know if I reached it? I became more contented and successful when I started describing my financial and other personal goals in a positive way. Two examples of goals I have held true to are: remain open to learning throughout my life, and provide financial stability to my family and a good education to my children. Give it a try – it really does work! Studies prove time and again that we get what we focus on.

A few earning money thoughts

In the career coaching I do, across all age groups, I frequently hear: 'I will do that job I love when I have enough money that I don't have to worry' or 'I will earn a lot in that job and then I can do XYZ'.

Maybe it has always been the case, but it feels to me that in general we are more worried – yes, worried – about how much money we *want*. Few people tell me how much money they *need*. Studies show that, whatever the amount you aspire to earning, it will just keep getting bigger as you achieve it. You'll never actually get to the number you think you want. So stop stressing about it! Once you understand that, life becomes easier, because it helps you realize it isn't about the money. Other things matter more; think about your happiest moments in life so far. What made them so special? Was it really about the money?

I wanted to share a few, perhaps somewhat random, money-related thoughts that may be useful to you now or later:

- **Is money a motivator or demotivator, satisfier or dissatisfier?** This is a huge topic, so I'll just summarize it here. Many studies have been done aimed at figuring out if money can be used as an incentive to get people to do things. In your case, did your parents offer you money if you earned certain grades at school? Did it work; did you study harder because of it? How did you feel if you didn't get the grades and didn't receive any money; and how did you feel if your brother or sister did?

  Psychologists have found that once a person's basic needs are met, getting more money, on its own, stops being a motivator.

- **Money gives you freedom** – you may think that once you earn lots of money you will have the freedom to choose how you spend your time. You may be able to pay other people to do the things you find mundane. That may be true, but do consider that you probably made some sacrifices of your freedom while you pursued your money goal – so you did pay a price for that freedom.

- **Money expands your horizons** – having money can lead to new and interesting experiences if you seek them out. By the same token, though, you can expand your horizons while spending very little. Learning is easy – read a book, take a course, go to a museum, go to free concerts. Travel options vary hugely: accommodation from a 6-star hotel down to a shared room in a youth hostel and everything in between; from Michelin-starred restaurants to market stalls.

- **Money will make you happy** – I don't want to overplay this, but I can't help but point out that despite what feels like a societal view that more is better, it just cannot be true. If it were, it would mean that richer people would always be happier than poorer people. We all know that's not the case. Beyond meeting basic needs, are you happier simply because you have more money in your pocket or bank account? I don't think so.

There is plenty of evidence that shows that lots of money doesn't lead to happiness. Think of the celebrities, talented musicians and other famous people whose lives ended early. Money didn't help them be happy, did it? One thing we know for sure – money doesn't protect you from the possibility of unhappy events. Those things are just part of life.

- **Charitable acts are a winner** – studies show that the most uplifting thing we can each do to gain short- and long-term satisfaction is to do something that helps others. Think about how you feel when you perform a simple act of kindness – even just a smile, holding the door open for someone, putting a small bit of money into a collection tin.

  Spending time on a charitable cause is recommended for people who have lost their jobs, lost loved ones or are suffering from depression. If you can combine your personal interests with a charitable cause, you're really onto a winner. Time and money focused in one place is impactful – take a look at what Bill Gates and Warren Buffet have managed to do. They are extremely wealthy, but we don't have to be wealthy in order to spend a bit of time and money to make a difference.

Lots of food for thought here. I hope the message comes through that, at the end of the day, it is all about *you*. Set your financial targets within a greater context of your life – money is only one element, so avoid making it overly important.

> 'Behind every overnight success lies years of hard work and sweat.'
>
> Often quoted, never attributed

'Now' decisions with a long-term earnings impact

You have already made decisions that will impact your long-term earnings potential and you will continue to do so. One of the most important is whether you have applied yourself at school and made the most of your education. I want to pause for one moment on this, though – the academic process and structure does not suit everyone. Some really smart young people I know did not get great grades at school or university and have gone on to have successful careers. Some just didn't fit in with the system, some just couldn't do exams, and some had learning difficulties (dyslexia for example seems to affect intelligent people). What they did not do is become disruptive in class; I recommend you avoid doing anything that might cause you to become labelled a 'troublemaker'.

The two most significant decisions for you now will be whether to continue your education post sixth form, and picking your first job, which may become your career.

Post-GCSE or sixth-form education

Wherever you are in your academic career, I encourage you to apply yourself – learning to learn is a great thing, so don't let the ongoing testing wear you down! In general, a strong academic record, in whatever formal education you complete, will open more doors than a poor academic record. I'm not saying that is fair, but that is the way it is. Some people really struggle with academia, owing to dyslexia or other disadvantages, but then find their niche and have fantastic careers; it's just harder work. Successful dyslexics include Richard Branson of Virgin fame, Florence Welch of Florence and the Machine, and Orlando Bloom, the famous actor. If, like them, academia is not your thing, my advice is to get out and get working as soon as you can. I've seen young people in similar situations feel pressured by parents and friends to go on to further study and then drop out without completing their course, as it was just too hard and frustrating. That did nothing for their self-esteem!

Attending university is not for everyone. Things to consider as you make your decision include:

1 the cost of university (tuition of £9,250 per year plus living costs, which will double the price);

2 the expansion in the number and breadth of offerings from vocational colleges, and recognition of the excellent career options they provide; and

3 the expansion of apprenticeship programmes.

Many companies that have been doing most of their recruiting at universities are now rethinking that strategy and offering apprenticeships for post-GCSE and post-sixth-form students, and other entry-level positions. These opportunities are across a wide range of careers, including plumbing, accountancy, beauty and banking. The UK government is encouraging firms to set up and expand apprenticeship programmes through its Apprenticeship Levy, which requires firms to pay the government a percentage of their wage bill. This percentage is then paid back to the firms for each apprentice they take on.

Did you know?

In a recent study, plumbers were deemed to be in the happiest profession. No university degree needed for that! But you do need to have an aptitude for it.

Vocational colleges are increasing their marketing efforts; these are available to post-GCSE and post-sixth-form students. Read the Sunday papers and use the internet to learn more about your options. The colleges are building strong relationships with employers, so they offer a great opportunity to get real-world experience – something employers are keen on! If you do well at your college course and at your work experience gained through that, your career will be off to a great start!

Yes or no to university

University was fully funded by the government across the UK until 1998. Over time more universities started charging students, and since 2016 the annual tuition fee in England and Wales has been £9,250. In Scotland, for Scottish students, the government continues to fully fund university – in other words, students do not pay tuition fees. Living expenses, if you don't live at home, are also substantial, although some of those may be covered by a grant. It will be difficult for most families to cover these expenses, so the level of student debt by the time of graduation is expected to increase. On average, university graduates are leaving with £27,000 of debt. (Take a look at Chapter 10 to learn more about university student loans.)

With the amounts of money at stake, young people need to think hard about whether or not university is right for them at this time in their lives. The financial implications of that decision *need* to be considered. Bear in mind that you can work to save money to fund going to university a few years later, and you can work while you are attending university.

There are careers that will continue to require a university education, and many of these frequently provide higher income levels. If you do decide to go to university, make sure you make your investment count. Picking the right university and course is important. As you do that, give thought to how you will use your degree when you leave university. You're there to learn… but equally importantly, you're there to launch your working career!

Working hard once you get to university is also important. Whatever you hear from others, the results from your first year *do* matter. If you want to apply for internships during the summers after your first and second years (which I recommend), you will be asked what your grades are so far. Anything below a 2:1 is unlikely to be good enough. I'm not saying you won't find something; what I am saying is that you are making it much harder for yourself as a result. Similarly, finishing your course with anything less than a 2:1 will make finding a job difficult, as many firms won't let you access their online application system without that result.

When you are applying, ask the university questions such as 'what percentage of your graduates get graduate-level jobs?'; 'what percentage of students have those lined up before graduation day?'; and 'what does the university do to help students get jobs?' Since 2013, universities have been required to publish the percentage of students, by course, who have secured jobs upon graduation.

First job and possible career choice

For most people, a career is what they see when they are middle-aged and they look back at the jobs they have held and find their 'story'. There are a minority of people who know (or think they know) what they want to do for their work lifetime when they are deciding on GCSE or A-level subjects. And a few more people get clearer when the time comes to apply for university. But in my experience, having coached hundreds of people at a variety of career stages, few people *really* know, and their career becomes one of exploration and opportunities. So don't feel pressured into making a lifetime decision about what you are going to do. There are many opportunities that will present themselves that haven't even crossed your mind yet; the key is to do great things at every job you take on and stay open-minded.

When you are thinking about your first job and where it could lead in terms of earnings, it's often easy to find out. You can go online, look at job advertisements or look through career books. As you do your digging, consider entry-level jobs and longer-term jobs in that area of interest, so you can get a feel for the senior jobs' earnings potential. Some jobs are higher paid than others, but be careful to consider the average, or expected, rate of pay, not the pay for superstars.

Typically, professions that require a big investment in education will pay more – think lawyers, investment bankers, doctors. If you are a star in any of those, you may make seriously big money. Sadly, some professions are not as well paid, such as teachers; but teachers do have the benefit of long holidays, which the first professions I mentioned do not. Nursing is another career that, despite its impact on society, does not generally pay terribly well. People in trades such as plumbers, builders and electricians seem to make a good living and have the flexibility (and risks) of probably running their own business. A recent study showed that people in these latter professions had the highest level of work/life satisfaction! In a nutshell, every career path has good stuff and bad stuff. What is important is to find a job that involves you in something you are interested in, and that will involve you doing something you are good at. That's because you'll be doing a lot of it!

As you consider careers and first jobs, in addition to the above, I suggest you think about the environment you'll be working in. Think through some basic questions about your likes and dislikes, along the lines of those in the box below.

Work environment preference questions

Do you…

- Want to work inside a building or outside?
- Prefer working with other people or on your own?
- Prefer working with computers or people?
- Like a routine where you go to the same place at the same time most days, or do you like to have a changing or unpredictable schedule?
- Have a preference for the ages of the people you work with?
- Like working with numbers or words?

There are many sources of advice if you search the internet. My advice? Just get going with the working and earning money and see where it leads you. If you have to stack shelves or pick vegetables, just do it! Once you are eligible to work, get a job working summers and/or evenings rather than hanging out at home. Be a 'mucker-inner' once you get a job – a positive 'do whatever I can to help' attitude goes a long way.

Keeping pace with the changing world

As you develop your career and financial aspirations, always keep an eye on what is happening in the world around you. Consider: What are the changes in the industry you're in? What's the impact of technology going to be? Is artificial intelligence going to impact what you do? Are there more competitors entering your market? What are your prospects for the future?

The questions above are very specific to you, so what about the bigger world? What's happening in the UK? And what about other geographies? Do they pose opportunities? Or are they threats to what you do? Do you want to live in another country?

How do you manage your personal development and increase the depth and breadth of your knowledge and competencies? Are you taking courses on technical matters? Management? Leadership? Data analytics? Coding? Are you taking MOOCs (Massive Online Open Courses offered by top universities around the world for free)?

No one is ever going to be more interested in your personal development than you – so pay attention to the world around you and the opportunities that arise. And if an opportunity arises to move to a new city or country – my personal recommendation is to always say yes!

TIP

Teenage job hunters, consider applying here: Marks & Spencer, Caffé Nero, Co-op, Sainsbury's, Tesco, Waitrose, McDonald's.

Take control of your earnings destiny

We've covered a lot of ground here. The thing is, unless you are planning to be supported by the government or a family member, you're going to have to support yourself. And that will mean making decisions about education, finding a job and creating your career. The decisions you make *now* about university and jobs will have an impact on your long-term earnings potential, so consider your financial aspirations as you make those decisions.

But it's not the full picture – keep in mind, too, the importance of your happiness, freedom and personal interests.

The skills you're learning now about managing your money will put you in a good position to reach your goals and be prepared for whatever your life holds in terms of career and financial situations. So, give yourself time to think about these things, set your aspirations and go for it! Planning now will help make sure you don't have any regrets later.

04
Spending money

The purpose of this chapter is to increase your awareness about your spending decisions. That will help you make smarter money choices – decisions that ensure you spend your money on what you *really want*, not just what you *want right now*. Maybe after reading this you'll consider 'If I do this with my money now, what might I be giving up tomorrow or next week?' You want to always, or nearly always, be able to think 'Yes, I made the right money decisions' – even in hindsight.

The reality of spending is that it is very easy to spend without thinking much about it. Once you start tracking what you spend, and budgeting, you will become more aware. I was told by most people that they started paying attention to their spending once they were earning their own money to support themselves. They started thinking harder about the cost of things – 'one beer is two hours of work' or 'a pair of shoes is two days' work'. Those sorts of thoughts will focus your mind!

Small spends add up

If you concentrate on your daily small spends, you can see how they add up to a lot of money. Here are a few examples that might be relevant to you:

- Daily coffee – £2.10 twice a day, 300 days per year, costs you £1,260 a year (probably after tax). Could you bring the cost down by going to a local shop rather than one of the big brands? How much would it cost you if you made your own coffee?

- Mobile phone – you 'have to have' the latest handset, or you upgrade regularly. How much do you spend on usage each month/year?

- Cinema visits – how often do you go? At £12 to watch the film plus popcorn and a drink, how much does each trip cost you?

- Pubs and restaurants – you may be surprised at how much you spend every month or week at these. What do you think you spend? Are you okay with that figure?

- Grabbing lunches – at £5 a day for a meal deal or other lunch, you will spend roughly £1,800 a year if you buy it seven days a week. What else could you do?

What do you think you spend your money on? Any idea what that looks like if you look at a year? Or per month? Do you think it changes much from month to month? What portion of your spending is fixed – rent, utilities, education – and what varies – gifts, clothes, meals out, drinks? This is all useful information for you to get to grips with.

Immediate gratification

Between your generation and the previous one, the speed with which you can get things you want has increased dramatically. You can watch any film you want at any moment; you can talk to anyone in the world from anywhere in the world at any time; you can access your e-mail at any time from anywhere; your smartphone (once the domain of senior business executives) means you are in touch all the time. Everything is instantaneous! How great is that?

Well, there can be downsides to everything being instant and to making instant decisions, because with hindsight they may not seem so great. Have you ever spent money on something and then wished you hadn't? Most of us have – in fact I still do from time to time when I'm in a hurry and something is on sale!

Quite often, if you slow down, pause and think, you will make a better decision. 'Better' here means more in line with what *you* really want.

'Too many people spend money they haven't earned, to buy things they don't want, to impress people they don't like.'

Will Rogers, actor, *The Week*

'Good' and 'not so good' spending

I collected stories of spending decisions that people around your age were happy and unhappy about. I also did quite a bit of eavesdropping on conversations. Here are a few of my findings:

- Frequent first memories of money, which we touched on earlier, included having money to spend on sweets and receiving pocket money for being good.

- Nearly everyone had a story about saving money for something, giving up things to be able to buy something they really wanted. They all remembered the feeling of success when they bought their special something.

- Everyone had 'wasted money' stories about shoes, clothes, mobile phones and other stuff they bought in haste and regretted later.

- One funny story – someone paid for a fairly expensive item with one-penny coins he had saved up.

Despite all the immediate gratification that people talk about, your generation also told me, when I conducted a survey, that they want to be financially independent – and *soon*. The best way to do that is to slow down and make thoughtful decisions.

Here are a few stories that may resonate with you:

- My daughter 'had' to have a Furby (an electronic robotic toy which was a 'must-have' a few years ago), so we traipsed all over London trying to find one as they were in huge demand. We finally found one and she spent all the money she had saved up from multiple birthdays. Once she got the Furby home, it was so annoying that it was banished to the cupboard within a month. It turned up 10 years later when we cleaned out the cupboard and was quickly banished to the attic. Have you ever spent money you saved for ages on something you then didn't even like?

- Maybe you bought a car – a good one at a really good price. But you found you didn't use it often and, when you did, there always seemed to be something wrong with it – a flat tyre, a slipping clutch. And parking it was a nightmare. In the end you may have regretted buying it in the first place.

- You splashed out on a really nice pair of shoes, a dress or a shirt for some special event. Afterwards you thought about the fact that no one said anything about it, the event was cancelled, it rained and your item got ruined, or you decided not to wear it as it 'didn't go with other things'.

- You bought something at a fabulous discount on sale. A great bargain. You didn't bother trying it on. Then, when you got it home, it was a poor fit, or you decided you just didn't feel comfortable in it, so you never wore it. You felt you wasted money when you started off thinking you were saving it.

- You got roped into a holiday plan that was well beyond what you planned to spend. Maybe it was because the group you were going with had more money than you, or they were just that bit older and earning more than you. Maybe you managed to cobble the money together to go on the holiday, but every time you did something during it, you were stressed as it was one more thing you 'couldn't really afford'.

- You went out for a meal with your friends. You didn't talk about how to split the bill, but you assumed you'd each pay for what you ordered (roughly). When the bill came someone suggested an even split. You didn't want to raise a fuss, even though you had chosen what to eat with your wallet in mind and knew it was going to financially stretch you to make up for it somehow. And on top of it you left the restaurant hungry!

Maybe a few of these sound familiar or maybe you have your own stories. Remember that your spending goal is to have 'no regrets', or better yet, the flip side – 'conscious, in-control spending' all the time.

'Britons waste about £360 each year, £17.6 billion, on buying food they could make themselves, take-out coffees, and paying interest on credit cards.'

Go Compare

Pause and reflect

Making conscious, in-control spending decisions requires just one thing. It requires you to avoid making snap decisions in the heat of a potential spending moment, choosing instead to pause and reflect on what you are doing. I have taken suggestions made by interviewees and summarized them as questions below for you to work through:

- What spending decisions can you remember that, with hindsight, you wish you hadn't made? Take the time to jot a list of them down (now, not later). Then, go back to the list and think about how you could have handled those situations differently. You may want to talk them through with friends to see if they have other ideas.

- What are you spending your money on at the moment that surprises you? Look at the list at the beginning of this chapter. What is your own list of small spends that turn big?

- What do you think you can do to make your money go a little further? Think back to the days leading up to the last time you were stuck at home because you had no cash for a few days.

- Where could planning ahead have saved you money? Fertile ground for this one is travel arrangements, grocery shopping, cinema visits and coupon websites.

- How often do you lose track of your spending when you are out partying?

Give yourself some time to reflect on these and come up with your own questions to add to the list. The test will be whether the list helps you next time you are making a spend decision; keep testing it out and adjusting it as you go along. You may find that you get it down to just one or two questions, which makes it easy to use every time you are deciding whether or not to spend your money.

TIP

There are phone apps to help with splitting bills – look into Splitwise, Splitter and Plates.

Escape routes

Inevitably you will get stuck in awkward money situations, and the more financially diverse the group of people you spend time with, the more likely it is these will happen. That is totally fine, as long as you have a few coping mechanisms to help you. Here are a few ideas:

- By far the easiest thing to do is be non-committal. When you feel pressured into spending on something you aren't sure about or are already sure you don't want to but don't know how to say so, find a way to buy yourself some time. Do this by simply saying something like 'I want to think about that' or 'Can I come back tomorrow on that?' Then go away and decide what you really want for *you*.

- Another approach is to consider what will happen if you don't spend on whatever it is. How will you feel about it? Is it really that important? Is it worth it? Will a moment of awkwardness now make things easier in the future? What do you want to spend your money on instead? What pleasure will that give you?

- Try to anticipate and avoid tricky situations. Peer pressure is very hard to deal with, and I'm sorry to say it's something that will continue throughout your life. How often do you hear statements such as 'you have to come' and 'you don't want to miss out'? How can you get yourself out of those jams (when you want to) without feeling you look pathetic, or cheap, or different? Well, what's surprising is that despite the angst of standing up for yourself in these situations, they do pass very quickly – and friends don't tend to hold it against you. It is very unusual for people to push someone hard into doing something once they have had the courage to firmly say 'no, thanks' or 'can't afford it'.

- Consider alternative ways to get the same result and suggest one of them. Think about how you can get the same outcomes for less. For example, have your beers in your room rather than the pub, or buy Pizza Express pizzas at the supermarket and cook them at home rather than going out to eat, or watch a sports match on TV rather than attend in person.

Think too about how you handle situations when you are the one trying to get people to spend money on something. How do you react when people hesitate to go along with your suggestion? Have you considered that maybe they are hesitating because they can't afford it? Do you make it easy for them to adjust your idea or say no?

There are lots of ways to enjoy life without spending much money. The internet is a real blessing when it comes to this, but you may have to break some old habits. Rather than thinking about going to an expensive club or out for a film, search the web for 'what's free in your city?' and 'things under £10'.

Missed opportunities

A lot of this chapter has been about managing your spending more carefully, and that implies spending less. While that was my bias, as so many of the young adults I spoke with wanted help with that, there is another side to controlling your spending: the times when you give lots of thought to something and decide not to spend your money on it at all. Maybe it's a good deal on a car, or tickets to a World Cup match or a holiday with friends. There's a chance that you'll regret the decision to *not* spend the money. One young man explained it really well when he said: 'My personal philosophy is that I take care and think hard about money decisions, but try every possible way not to let opportunities pass me by because of money.'

In a nutshell, *you* are in control of your spending, no one else, so take that control with gusto. Find ways to slow your spending decision making so that you make each decision within a bigger context. Setting spending targets will help you with that; we look at these in the next chapter. And remember – the goal is no regrets, whether you decide to spend or not!

05
Keeping in control of your money

As you know, the purpose of this book is to help you control your money; to help you make decisions you are happy with, both when you make them and when you look back on them at some time in the future. Based upon my discussions, the biggest regret young people have (well, maybe all ages) is that they spent too much money. For some, that meant they spent more than they wanted to; for others it was more than they could actually afford to, or more money than they had; and for most it was a series of spends that they wished they'd not made. To be fair, every one of us will make a poor financial decision at some point – we just want to make sure the impact is not huge.

A key to keeping yourself in check is to know what money has come in and out, and comparing those figures with what you 'hoped' for. In this chapter we will look at how turn those 'hopes' into a 'budget': which is just a money plan with target figures. We'll figure out how to collect detailed information about Money Ins and Outs, how to summarize that information into categories and then set a target figure for each category. And with that, you will have a budget. Simple!

What's a budget?

A budget is a plan. It shows you what money you plan/expect/hope (you choose the word that works for you) to get in. And it shows you what money you plan/expect/hope (again, your choice of word) to spend.

On the money coming *in* side, a budget helps you answer questions like: Where will your money come from and when? Did the money you actually receive match what you expected to receive? If you're on an annual salary, which becomes a monthly amount of pay, it's pretty easy to figure out what will come in once your tax code gets sorted out (see Chapter 8). If you are paid by the hour, the money will fluctuate because of the number of hours you work, whether you work overtime, and whether those hours are paid at different rates. If you are paid hourly, remember that you won't be paid for time taken away from work for holidays, doctor and dentist visits and being off sick. Ditto if you're a full-time contract worker.

When you get money in you have two choices – save it or spend it. We will focus mostly on the 'spend it' or money *out* option. A budget helps you understand: Did you spend your money the way you planned to? What would you like to spend your money on? What spending decisions do you make up front and what do you decide at the time of purchase? What took your spending off course and by how much?

Budgeting will also help you be better able to fund non-standard financial events from your ongoing cash flow, like holidays, presents and big nights out, and will help you avoid getting into debt for those. Your budget may even help you start to save money!

Reasons not to create a budget

Not convinced you need to do a budget yet? Maybe you have the same thoughts as others shared with me when I asked them about budgeting and they said it was a 'waste of time'. Here are examples of what I heard and my line of response:

- 'I don't know what I've spent my money on.' Exactly why you need a budget. You can't manage what you can't see.

- 'I don't have enough money to worry about budgeting.' Another good reason to have a budget. With one, you may find you have more money choices than you think.

- 'My parents control what I spend because they fund me and will top me up if I need it!' This may sound great, but at some point it may end in tears as your parents won't fund you forever. Learning to manage your money is an important life skill that, like many things, is easiest if learned early.

- 'I don't have the time.' This really means 'it's not important enough'. And it may not be, until you face a financial crisis or really want something that you could have had if only you had managed your money better.

When you read the comments above, they may or may not sound rational, but they definitely aren't consistent with controlling your money destiny. And controlling your money destiny is the reason you're reading this book. So, I encourage you to give budgeting a go – it really isn't that hard to get going, and you'll find it incredibly useful. I still do it!

Collecting your information

The critical factor to this process, and the usefulness of the output, is your diligence in collecting data. Take some time now to think about how you will collect your data – data about money coming *in* and going *out*. Your bank account will provide a lot of information, but you will need to supplement it with additional sources like payslips and credit card information (see Chapters 8 and 9 about financial basics). You will also have to track what cash you receive and pay – what were those amounts for? You may or may not do many cash transactions, probably quite few if you have a debit card and can tap for most purchases. But if you do use cash, you will need to keep track of what you're spending it on – perhaps by marking up the cash withdrawal slip, or by keeping your receipts for any cash payments.

Banks and other firms have developed technology solutions that can help you with spending data collection and analysis – useable on laptops and smartphones – but they all rely on you to review that information regularly and fix any classification issues (I do it about every 2–3 days because otherwise I forget what I spent money on). You will also have to track whatever you have spent on a credit/store card and classify that spending. There are a few apps that exist now, and others keep emerging, that will help you take your spending from your bank account automatically into your budget spreadsheet. These include IReconcile, Expenditure, MoneyBook, Mint, Quicken and Microsoft Money.

What a budget looks like

Let's pause for a moment and look at the end result of what you will be doing (Figure 5.1)

Figure 5.1 A complete budget

MY BUDGET

	January			February			Year to date	
	Actual	Target	Notes	Actual	Target	Notes	Actual	Target
MONEY IN								
Salary/hourly wages	1800							
Overtime wages	0							
Less taxes, NI, etc	110							
Other money in	20		Birthday					
TOTAL MONEY IN	1710	1600						
MONEY OUT								
Rent/mortgage payment	400	400						
Gas/water/electricity	70	70						
Phone/internet/technology	40	45						
Insurance	30	0						
Food	200	180						
Eating out	60	100						

MY BUDGET

	January			February			Year to date	
	Actual	Target	Notes	Actual	Target	Notes	Actual	Target
Entertainment	0	40						
Clothing	120	100						
Transportation	50	50						
Holidays	0	0						
Birthdays/gifts	30	15						
Other	50	100						
TOTAL MONEY OUT	**1050**	**1100**						
Total money in, less total money out	**660**	**500**						
Money into savings account	200							
Money elsewhere	300		Pay credit card					
Left in current account	**160**							

As you can see, this is a fairly simple document. All you are doing is capturing where money has come in from and where it has gone out to – the left-hand column. You also want to compare what actually happened to what you planned to have happen – the 'actual' and 'target' for a month. There is also a column for notes so you can leave yourself a reminder of what has happened.

Take a look at the 'January Actual' column in conjunction with the categories. I have suggested a list of categories for types of money coming **in** and going **out**. You can use what I have done or create your own categories. To figure out the categories you need, I suggest you start with what you think your list should be and then see if your month's money activities fit into the categories. If not, just add a category.

You'll see that there's an 'other' category for each of Money In and Money Out, which is where you put money that doesn't fit anywhere else. If the number in that category gets big, relative to the other amounts, take a look at what is in it and see if you need some other categories in order for the spreadsheet to be useful. If you have a category that has zero in the first month, but you know you will need it later (eg weddings, holiday gifts) – keep the category in there. You can see how easy it is now to see where your money is coming from and where it is going.

Let's continue to the bottom of the spreadsheet. One of the most important reasons for creating a budget is to make sure that your Money In is greater than your Money Out. The easiest way to get out of control and into big debt is to overspend! So, to highlight the net Ins/Outs, have a space as shown for Total Money In, Less Total Money Out (Figure 5.2).

You can then decide what to do with what is (hopefully) left over. You can put it in your savings account – maybe saving for something special or to put into an ISA later – and if you want, put a note in the Notes column. You may want to allocate that money elsewhere – perhaps to a credit card balance, as this example shows. And the remainder sits in your current account.

Let's focus on the Target column. Remember that this is here to help you manage your money. You may want to start by just setting targets for the overall Money In or by each line item. In this example I have shown a total for Money In and an amount by Money Out category. You may choose to start with no targets, as you don't know enough about your money yet: that's totally fine. Armed with a few months' data, you will be able to set targets for total **Ins** (fairly easy) and total **Outs** (hard). Start with the total **Out** amount that you feel is right for you, relative to the **In**, and then set

Figure 5.2   Budget 2

	January			February			Year to date	
	Actual	Target	Notes	Actual	Target	Notes	Actual	Target
TOTAL MONEY OUT	1050	1100						
Total money in, less total money out	660	500						
Money into savings account	200							
Money elsewhere	300		Pay credit card					
Left in current account	160							

targets for each category. *Be realistic!* If your spending shows that you're spending £300 a week eating out, setting a next month target of £0 is probably a push too far. Decide what you think is the right number, the number *you* are happy with. As you can see, I have put in only a total Money In target figure. The reason for that is I figured I couldn't do much about the Ins so why bother trying to be more specific? But for the Outs I have set targets by item as that would be helpful to me.

Each month, you'll input your Money In and Out information; you can then compare the *actual* to the *target* amounts to see how you've done. Use the Notes column to add anything you want to be able to remember that will influence your next month. That can be thoughts on both the actual and target. For example, if you want to spend nothing on clothes for a few months, put a comment in the Notes column to remind you. If you like, you can add a column that shows the difference between the month's Actual and Target amounts.

It is useful to keep a running total of target and actual amounts (this is what the Year to Date column is for), so that you can easily see how you're doing overall. This will also be helpful as you set your plan for the next year.

However you use your budget, I would encourage you to use the bottom four line items on this example, and include targets for them as well. Having a savings target is important, but remember that paying off debt that costs you money is a higher priority. (Having said that, do make sure you have some cash on hand as unexpected things can happen.)

Let's now go into this in greater detail. I'll assume that you're using a debit card, and an app that provides you with money spent that you can categorize and upload into your spreadsheet.

Budget step one: collect detailed money information

To do this, you'll need information from your bank, payslips and credit card statements. You'll also need to track money Ins and Outs that aren't captured by these; for example, your bank app won't provide details of where 'cash withdrawal' money goes, so you'll need to collect and input that.

If you don't go for the technological approach, keep a money diary or list somewhere in whatever way works for you. Every item needs to have a date, an amount, what type of transaction it was (cash, credit card, debit card, Apple Pay, store card) and an explanation of what the payment or receipt of money was for. You may want to record everything in a notebook, or you might like to track things on scrap paper or receipts, or you may want to log the data directly onto a spreadsheet as you go. (I prefer the scrap paper and receipt approach, personally, but whatever you do, remember to keep this information safe and organized!)

Tracking money coming **in** is usually relatively easy. These **Ins** include any allowance you receive, earnings from a job, birthday money, government money, and maybe other things. Include everything so you get the full picture.

When you get paid for work (monthly or weekly), your payslip will be your money spreadsheet source document. If your parents deposit money into your bank account, your bank statement will be your spreadsheet source document. If you are paid cash for work, you need to make a note of that straight away, including any tips you receive. If your pay has deductions for income tax and other things, use the details included on the payslip to reflect the total you earned as money coming in, and the total monies deducted. In the spreadsheet set the formula so that Total Money In is Salary/Hourly wages plus Overtime wages, less Taxes, NI, etc plus Other Money In.

Tracking money going **out** is harder than tracking money coming in, because there are many more transactions. For the money going out from your bank account, you'll need to review transactions, classify them and upload them into your spreadsheet.

Figure 5.3   Credit, debit and cash spending

January spending				
	Credit card	**Debit card**	**Cash**	**Total**
Rent/Mortgage payment				
Gas/Water/Electricity				
Phone/Internet/Technology				
Insurance				
Food				
Eating out				
Entertainment				
Clothing				
Transportation				
Holidays				
Birthdays/Gifts				
Other				
Total				

There are several other source documents that will be the basis for entries into your money spreadsheet. In order to make sure you don't miss anything, you may find it helpful to create a separate spreadsheet (or notebook, or whatever works for you) for every month, so you can work out what you've spent, where you've spent it and *how* you've spent it. Figure 5.3 shows an example of what one month's spreadsheet might look like.

As you can see, the rows match up with the Money Out categories on our main budget – this is a good way to work out the accurate totals for a really useful monthly budget. Here is some information about them with a few tips for each:

- **Cash machine withdrawal slips** – every time you get cash out, get a receipt and write on it what you spent the money on. You may have to carry that receipt around for a bit as you may not spend the money immediately. Keep the receipts in a place where you can find them when you go to record your money outflows.

- One of the biggest gaps in spending records is when you go out for a night and get £20 out of the cash machine on the way out, forgetting your process. It's also easy to forget to record money you withdraw during your night out. I can't tell you how many times I have heard someone complain that 'someone took their money' or they 'lost their money' on those sorts of nights. So get the slip, stick it in your pocket or wallet so that you remember you got money out, and mark it up the next day.

- **Bank account statement** – bank accounts, including what is processed through your current account (eg debit card transactions, which include 'contactless' payments), are explained in Chapter 9, so you may want to read through that section now. Because nearly all of your money-related activities will sooner or later flow through your bank account, it is a great source of information. Every time you get cash from a money machine, check your account balance to make sure it is in line with what you expect. Then every few days or at least once a week, review the transactions and make sure the system has classified them correctly – the machine will learn! If there is an entry you don't recognize, investigate it immediately.

Debits and credits

The balance in your bank account decreases with debits and increases with credits. Debits include direct debits, standing orders and transactions you made with your bank debit card, including cash machine withdrawals. Credits include deposits into your account, the most frequent being payments received from your employer, money deposited by your parents and any cheques you deposited.

- **Credit card statement** – every month, each credit card provider will send you a monthly statement via the post and/or e-mail. Credit cards are covered in detail in Chapter 9, so either read that now or just focus on tracking spending. The monthly statement will include the beginning balance, every transaction, and the ending balance. What you need to do for money outgoing tracking purposes is analyse every entry and allocate each to a budget category.

- I recommend that every time you use the card, you get a receipt, immediately write on it what you bought, and put it in an envelope somewhere.

You may think you don't need to do this because you'll remember what you spent your money on… but it's very hard to remember after the fact. To add to the difficulty, sometimes the name of the shop you bought the item from is not the same as the one that appears on the credit card receipt. When your credit card statement comes, take out your envelope of receipts and tick them off against the statement, marking on the statement the budget category that each amount relates to. If you have used a contactless card, you may or may not have had the option to receive a receipt. If not, make a note somewhere of the spend, what it was for and the date.

- Account for *every item*, even very small ones. Fraudsters make a lot of money from people by charging small amounts to lots of people regularly. If you don't think you should have been charged for something, ring the credit card company immediately.

- Once you have accounted for every item on the statement, calculate the total amount of money that has gone out for each budget category of your spreadsheet. Make sure that the grand total of your individual category totals is the same figure as the total monthly credits shown on the credit card statement. Were you charged interest? If so, this will show up on the statement and needs to be captured on your summary as a Money Out Other – unless this is a big number which you want to capture separately.

- **Debit card statement** – there is no such thing as a debit card statement. Every time you use your debit card, the money goes out of your account immediately and will appear on your bank statement.

- **Store card statement** – this is the same as when you use a credit card.

- **Apple Pay, Samsung Pay, Android Pay or other payment app statement** – you won't receive a statement of goods you paid for with your contactless payment app. When you register for the application, you'll be asked where the money you use should be taken from. You either direct it to your current bank account or to a credit card, which means your app usage will be reflected in your bank or credit card statement.

Budget step two: fill in your money spreadsheet

I'll assume here that you're using technology to collect bank account information and automatically load it into your spreadsheet. That should automate about 80 per cent of this process but the amount of ease it provides will vary. Even if you have to do all the input manually, it's worth the effort!

Take all the source documents you have collected. I start with any pay-slips and other work-related documents, followed by bank-account-related receipts (cash machine and direct debit advice slips and receipts), then my bank statement and then my credit card statements.

- Starting with payslips, put in your gross pay, deductions and net pay. If you are on hourly wages, I suggest separating the money you earn at regular pay rates from your overtime pay, if that applies.

- Turn to your bank account statement. Assuming you have been tracking your entries during the month, the information you load should be complete on the Money Out side. I recommend scrolling through the month's entries, item by item, on the system and making sure you are happy with their classification. Then look at the credits (Money In) to your account. These may have been captured in the classification system, but maybe not, so make sure they are entered into your spreadsheet.

- Next comes your credit and store card statements. Put the total amount by category into the spreadsheet. You can see why you may want the additional spreadsheet shown above.

- Next, total the entries – if you are using the extra spreadsheet for source of entry (cash, bank account etc), take the total from this to work out the monthly Actual figure.

- Finally, assuming you have set targets, calculate the difference between the monthly totals by category and the target amounts. Have the spreadsheet show clearly where the amounts are more versus less than the target.

That is your data collected and entered into the spreadsheet. It's likely to take quite a bit of time to do this for the first few months, but it will quickly get fast and easy.

Budget step three: begin exploring and understanding your money reality

Now you can start the interesting part of looking at the information you collected and asking yourself a bunch of questions. Just a few to start:

- Are you happy with the general story of what is coming in and going out?
- Does it show what you expected? What do you see that is surprising (good and bad news on this one)?

- Do you wish you had spent your money differently? What was 'worth it' and 'not worth it' in hindsight?
- What is your leftover figure? What could that figure have been?
- What do you think of the In and Out category totals?
- What do you think about your targets? Are they right or do they need adjustment?
- Is there anything you want to do differently on the Ins?
- Where could you reduce the Outs? Pick out a few items that you want to change or think about changing.
- Thinking about making changes going forward, which of these will be a challenge to change? Which will be easy?
- What would it take to get the total In and Out numbers to match? Or to have money left over?

More about setting budget targets

A target is a number you set for each In and Out category (and overall) that you would *like* the number to be. It's the figure you are going to work towards, not necessarily what you'll achieve straight away.

You may want to spend a few months learning about your money patterns before you make decisions on targets. But, if in the first month your Outs are larger than your Ins, you need to at least set an overall Out target and decide what you will spend less money on in the coming month. Remember, this is about you being in control of your money, so deciding what you want your money situation to look like is what you're aiming for.

Money In

How do the actual figures look? In total *and* by each component? How much of it is certain to come in and how much is hopeful? Where is that money coming from? Is it from your parents, from work or somewhere else? Is it from student loans or other educational subsidies?

You can have a column on your spreadsheet for notes you want to make about specific targets. For example, you may want to make a note that in a specific month when you can work full-time, the number will be bigger.

Chances are that, at this stage of life, the Money In part of your budget will be fairly straightforward, but it's still worth focusing on. If you consider working more to increase your Money In, remember to consider what impact that may have on your long-term aspirations. If you're already busy with lots going on in your life, including studies, what will be the impact of taking on more work? It can sometimes be easier to reduce your spending than boost your earnings in order not to jeopardize your long-term goals.

Money Out

Follow the same process for these figures as you did for Money In. It's probably going to be harder to do than the In was. Ask yourself some questions about what you see so far and what you would like to see. What do your actual figures look like? What's surprising about them – which are you happy with and which do you want to change? What do you want to spend your money on going forward?

What's your number?

- How many pub trips or drinks a week is reasonable?
- How much per week on eating out or socializing is reasonable?
- What do you think you need to spend on transport?
- What is reasonable to spend on clothes in a month?
- How much do you really want to spend on watching or doing sport?

Think about the little things you could do to reduce your spending in ways that wouldn't be huge inconveniences. A few things others have suggested include:

- Avoid ever buying a ticket on London transport (this may be true in other cities as well). You can either use a contactless card or an Oyster card (issued by Transport for London). Make sure you tap in and out on the same card and use the same card during a 24-hour period. If you are under 18 (16 or 17), you are eligible for a 16+ Zip Oyster photocard, which gives you discounts of up to 50 per cent on normal transportation rates.

If you live in a London borough, it also gives you free bus travel. Visit www.tfl.gov.uk for up-to-date information. For those of you not in London, check your local transportation website for information.

- How much do you have to spend on your car or motorcycle? How can you reduce that figure? What about driving more slowly? And revving the engine less? (Annoyingly, this has been pointed out to me!)

- Plan ahead when you're going to make a trip by train and do the same for flights.

- When you do eat out, go somewhere where you can use a coupon, or where they have a special deal.

- Make your own lunch to take to university, work or school.

- Invite friends around for drinks and ask them to bring their own. That's always less costly than drinks out – over £4 for a pint of beer out, compared with £1.50 for a bottle of beer at home.

- Do the same for meals. Don't go out; get everyone to share or take turns cooking.

- Cut clothes purchases to zero. Only buy when you really *really* need it, not just because it's on sale, is easy to buy off the net, or is cheap. The most frequently cited waste of money I heard about was spending money on unneeded clothes.

Think too about where you need to put in a figure that is larger than your current month's analysis shows. Are there any categories that were unusually low and don't reflect reality? Perhaps you were busy studying for exams so you didn't have much time to spend money. Perhaps you had no big birthday parties to go to – no travel, no presents – but a few are coming up.

Money In less Money Out

As you went through the process described above, you probably kept an eye on the In minus Out figure at the bottom of the spreadsheet. Now take a closer look at that.

Did you get a positive number? Great! Is that what you expected? Maybe you're already putting money aside for something big coming up; or you're a saver; or you're working to pay off an overdraft, credit card balance or store card balance. Or was it just a lucky month where you worked extra hours and earned more than usual, or you spent less than usual?

Did you get a negative number? NOT a good outcome. Take a look at why. Were your Ins unusually low for the month, or your Outs unusually high? Or was it a typical month? Look again at the Money In and then the Money Out by category to see what you can do to at least break even every month.

Obviously, if the total Outs are bigger than the total Ins every month, you're going to get into a big hole. That clearly isn't what you want, so go back again and get tougher with yourself. The worst thing to get stuck into at your age is a huge debt spiral. Whatever mechanism you're using to fund your current lifestyle, such as overdrafts, you *will* have to pay it back!

Remember a savings target

Most of the people I spoke with were just trying to make ends meet, so not even thinking about saving money. I understand that situation for people still in education or not earning much money – if this is you, that's okay.

What I *couldn't* understand was the people earning quite a bit of money and still spending everything that came in, as if it would just keep arriving. Some of the jobs they were doing did not guarantee that steady stream of income for the longer term. What did the higher earners spend it on? Fancy restaurants, pricey holidays and expensive clothes. They explained this at the same time as they were telling me that they were worried about saving money to buy a car or a home. They hadn't thought about this saving thing. Of course I gave them a few ideas!

You can start saving as soon as you want to – even if it's just a few coins a week. In practice, though, you'll most likely start saving when you need to. I bet that you've probably already done this without thinking of it as saving. Maybe you wanted to have money for an end-of-term holiday, to travel during a pre/post-university gap year, or you wanted to buy a piece of equipment for a hobby, or you wanted to buy a bike or a car, or you had a bunch of 21st birthday parties coming up. Those types of events probably made you save money, at least for a bit. I encourage you to take a read through Chapter 6, which has practical ideas on how to save.

Your money, your way

Well, there you are! You now have a budget. Keep in mind that the purpose of this budget is to help *you* manage your money, so get the system to work for you. The amount of effort you'll have to put into meeting your *in*, *out* and *save* targets will depend on how much you want to change what you currently do. You may have decided to change things radically, or opted to just tinker around the edges, depending on your past and current financial situation. At this stage of life, chances are that the changes you're trying to make are focused on the Out categories.

Changing money habits, like other habits, can be really hard at first. But changing a money habit you have chosen to change can be really satisfying. It's just like meeting other challenges you set for yourself – in sport and in your studies. I really encourage you to stick with it. If you focus on short-term money management and your long-term financial aspirations, your chance of success is really high.

If the changes you're trying to make are really hard, try these simple tricks to help you:

- Ask your friends for help. Tell them what you're working on and get them to be tough with you if they see you doing things that are inconsistent with the goals you explained to them.

- Keep a crib sheet in your wallet of the categories with tough targets, and keep a note of what you spend as you go along, so you always know where you are in relation to that target.

- Put a Post-it note on your credit and debit cards saying 'Do I need it?'

Keep your tracking and targeting going... forever

Having done all this work, you want to keep it going. Collecting the Money In and Out data on an ongoing basis is *critical*, as is the monthly review of actuals versus your targets. Early on, or if your money is tight, you may want to do your review fairly frequently. If money isn't so tight, and once you get the hang of your 'normal' money patterns, you may not feel the need to do it too often.

What does this periodic review involve? As you review the numbers, the fundamental decision you need to make is: if there is a gap between the actual and target figures, is it due to an inappropriate target that should be adjusted, or is it due to behaviour inconsistent (good or bad) with your plans when you set the target? If the actual and target numbers are the same, consider them too and think whether you want to change any of them.

Consider again your longer-term goals and consider whether you can adjust your spending to help you achieve them. Be really critical, for example how many meals out? How many coffees?

Keep your target history so you can reflect back on your successes over time. In the example at the beginning of the chapter, I've suggested tracking a *year to date* figure, so that you can look at a running total of how you're doing versus your plan. Now that the spreadsheet is set up, you can do all sorts of other analyses of averages, trends and whatever else you want.

If you keep doing this, you'll find that you pretty much know how you're doing versus your budget at any time. Your efforts at increasing awareness of what you do with your money will pay off, and by the time you get to the end of each month you'll be pretty sure if you are near your targets or not before you prepare your analysis. Having a nil balance in your bank account, being overdrawn or having cash in hand to move to a savings account won't come as a surprise. You'll know without having to look if your bank account is healthy or sickly.

Banking technology is coming to the rescue

In recent years there have been significant investments by established banks, new banks and buying discounts/cashback firms to help you manage your money more effectively and efficiently. Many banks will now help you avoid bank charges by sending you an alert (you can choose if it's via a text message or e-mail) when your cash balance is dangerously low and before you go overdrawn. As I mentioned above, many will provide an analysis of your spending and you can upload that into your spreadsheet. Offerings and support to customers will continue to change quickly, so keep talking with your friends about what they're using.

I am hearing more about people opening a second bank account where they transfer their monthly 'spending money' so they know they can't go over a fixed amount, or they transfer the money to a prepaid debit card. I want to be clear: I'm not personally recommending any of these companies or services – you should *always* do your due diligence when placing money with a new company, by looking at reviews, trusted money websites, and asking people you know.

The bank I hear of most often is Monzo, but others are following their example. They will send you a monthly report of what you have spent your money on, and there are no fees or charges. You can also use the same process when you go on holiday, and there are no charges for spending abroad. I have been told that the Monzo app is very user friendly. Keep an eye on Monzo, Starling and other emerging banks which are offering services to help you control your money better.

There are also new firms emerging which offer one or two services, such as Transferwise for currency payments, Wealthify for investments, and specialist mortgage companies. The offerings are emerging quickly, so always seek out the latest in the money sections of newspapers and on the web!

Technology solutions are also emerging that make it easier for you to receive cashback and discounts when you're making purchases. Two names that came up often (again, I am not recommending them) are Quidco and Curve. When you register with Quidco, you choose the places where you want to shop and you'll receive an alert when discounts are on offer. Curve is a prepaid credit card that gives you cashback; it also provides you with an analysis of what you spend your money on each month. It's possible to register any, or all, of your credit cards with Curve, and you'll receive cashback and a spend analysis for all of your cards.

And that leads to one drawback. If you use a combination of banks, cards and discount firms, you will have your spending information in a number of places, and you'll have to find a way to consolidate them in order to give yourself a full picture of your incomings and outgoings.

Managing your money

The budgeting process described above is going to put you **totally in control** of your money. You will know how much you earn and spend, and each time you make a money decision, you'll be able to do it based on facts. As you do this tracking, you may conclude that you can't match your Ins and Outs every month – and that's okay. There are a *lot* of variables, particularly around spending. It's hard, for example, to absorb big spends like holidays and parties into the monthly targets. This is where saving will help you – putting a bit aside regularly is an easy way to be ready for those bigger events. That isn't the way to fund the buying of a house or a car, but it's the easiest way to even out some of the smaller money needs you will have. The other way to meet short-term money needs is to go overdrawn, use your credit card or borrow money from somewhere – each of which has a cost, as explained in Chapter 7.

As you start looking to make bigger and longer-term decisions, this budget tool will also help. If you need to save for something big, like buying a house, paying for a wedding or going on a full gap year, take a different approach to the budget. Figure out what you absolutely *must* spend – cut out anything optional, anything that falls into the 'want' not 'need' bucket. This will show you just how much you can save. I read about someone who wanted to pay off credit card balances and bought *no* clothes, absolutely nothing, for a year. And someone told me about not buying coffees and lunches out every day, saving thousands of pounds in a year.

Your budget process and the help of your bank, and other firms' offerings, will help you take control of your money. The disciplines you put in place now will be habits of a lifetime, boosting your confidence in your ability to use your money the way *you* want to.

06
Saving and investing money

When I suggest to people that it is possible for most of us to save money, they often they tell me it is not possible. Once we work through their spending in detail we often find ways to squeeze out savings without too much pain. The key is to turn saving money into a habit, and the best way to do that is to start small. Small savings, put aside regularly, can turn into sizeable stashes of cash. In this chapter we will review a few ways to start saving and then explore what to do with it to turn those small savings into bigger money pots.

Ideas to help you start saving

- Use a glass money jar for general savings – for all coins or selected ones like pound coins.
- Save for a specific need and track your savings progress towards that goal – eg a holiday, a pair shoes or a deposit on a car.
- Make a graph of the amount of money in your savings account and put it on your wall.
- Set up a standing order to transfer a set amount of money weekly/monthly from your current bank account to a savings account.
- Transfer your 'spending allowance' to a separate bank account, one that provides an automated analysis of your spending.

It's very easy to get into the habit of spending all of the money you earn, particularly early in your career. One of the easiest opportunities to start saving is when you get a pay increase. Rather than spend that additional money, transfer the amount of that increase into a savings account of some sort. The point here is that 'little but often' works better for most of us than trying to set big amounts aside.

A useful savings goal is to have six months of 'spending' money in an account (preferably an interest-earning one that you can access freely) within a few years of starting work. This is to give you protection that if something happens and you can't earn money, or a surprise expense comes up, you will be prepared. One important caution – *before* saving, you need to pay off any short-term, high-interest debt like credit cards.

Did you know?

The *Daily Mail* says a survey by lending website RateSetter has found that 59 per cent of 18- to 30-year-olds would rather spend their wages on nights out, fashion and luxuries than saving for the future. This includes takeaways, meals out, clothing, television streaming services and cosmetics.

What to do with savings – key concepts and terminology

Once you have saved up some money, you will start to think about how to make that money make more money for you. As gratifying as it is to see the jar filling up by putting money in, it would be even better if it increased beyond what you put in! As you'll see, there is quite a bit of 'lingo' around investment opportunities, so I'll explain that as well.

Rate of return

When you save money, you want to be paid something for doing so. This is typically in the form of interest or dividends. The amount you earn divided by the money you put in is the rate of return, which is expressed as a percentage. If you earn a rate that is *greater* than the rate of inflation you're making economic headway. (Take a look at Chapter 2 to make sense of that comment.) But keep an eye on the level of risk you're taking (remember, higher risk = higher return), and your ability to get your money when you need it (see 'Liquidity' on the next page).

Annual equivalent rate (AER)

This number tells you the rate of interest you'll earn if you leave your money in an account/savings vehicle for a full year. The percentage rate is the interest you will receive divided by the money you have invested, annualized. Financial institutions calculate AERs by following a specific formula so it's easy for you to compare offerings. You may be paid interest monthly or annually, with annually being slightly better, although for small amounts it doesn't make much difference. It does matter for large sums. Unlike some other investments we will explore, with these you will know when you'll be paid interest and how much it will be.

TIP

If the rate of return on an account or investment looks too good to be true... it probably is! Avoid these completely!

Risk/reward principle

We looked at this in Chapter 2, and it comes up time and again in relation to any money decision. Keep this principle at the top of your mind when you're investing. If an investment opportunity has a return that looks great, you need to look at it carefully. Chances are it poses a high risk, which is fine as long as you understand the potential upside and downside. You'll see that any advertising or document related to an investment will have a prominent disclosure that states 'the value of this investment may go down as well as up'.

Liquidity

This is another critical concept when it comes to investing. What liquidity describes is how quickly you can turn your investment into cash. One of the reasons many bank savings accounts provide such a low rate of interest is that you can withdraw your money at any time without giving the bank any notice. The longer the period you commit to someone having your money, the more they will pay you for it. While you may be happy with a high rate of return, you won't be so happy if you can't access your money when you want it.

Even if you have committed to leaving your money in an investment for a set period, you can often still access it by paying a penalty fee. That penalty can easily wipe out any income previously received. Let me demonstrate what I mean by liquidity: investing money in a home is an attractive option for many reasons. What is *not* attractive is the fact that it can take time to sell the house, and that if you need the money you have invested in it, you can't turn it into cash quickly. As you can see, a home is an *illiquid* asset.

Did you know?

Sixty-seven per cent of consumers find choosing suitable financial products too complicated.

Investment-related taxes

One of the easiest ways to make your money work harder is to ensure your investment earnings are free of tax obligations. The government encourages savings through the personal savings allowance, which applies to interest earned, for example, in your bank account. The result is that a basic-rate taxpayer will be able to earn £1,000 of interest in a year from savings without paying tax. Higher-rate tax payers will be able to earn £500 tax-free. Additional-rate taxpayers will not be entitled to the personal savings allowance. In addition, if you invest money in shares/equities, the government currently allows you to earn dividends of up to £2,000 without paying taxes. Amounts more than that will be taxed at 7.5 per cent, 32.5 per cent and 38.1 per cent for basic-, higher- and additional-rate taxpayers, respectively. There are also tax benefits to setting up Individual Savings Accounts (ISAs) and making pension plan contributions, which are described in this chapter.

Any investment earnings will need to be included in your tax return, if you're required to file one, and if your investment earnings exceed the amounts described above.

You may also earn *gains* from investment transactions, for example you sell a share/stock for more than you paid for it. That increase in value is called a **capital gain** and will be taxed at a lower rate than earned income. Currently, you only have to pay tax on these if you make capital gains in excess of £12,000 during a tax year. (The sale of your home, and of any 'personal' asset, such as a car, for less than £6,000, is exempt from this tax.)

In general terms, capital gains that exceed the allowance will be taxed at a rate of 10 per cent for basic-rate taxpayers and 20 per cent for higher-rate taxpayers. If the asset you sold was a residential property other than your primary residence, the capital gains tax rate is 18 per cent for basic-rate taxpayers and 28 per cent for higher-rate taxpayers.

Fixed-term deposit

You're quite likely to hold the money you save with a bank. If it's held in an ordinary savings account, where you can get to it whenever you want, you won't get much interest. The next step up in terms of return and commitment is to put the money on *fixed-term deposit*, which is exactly what it sounds like: you commit to leaving a certain amount of money on deposit with your bank, or another financial institution, for a specified amount of time. In return for that commitment you'll be paid a higher rate of interest. The reason the institution is giving you a higher rate is that it can lend out your money to people who want to borrow money, and those borrowers will have to pay a higher rate of interest than the bank is paying you. If you withdraw your money before the agreed time, you'll be subject to a sizeable penalty. Note: you will frequently see these deposit offerings described as fixed-term bonds. (To avoid confusion we will separate these from what I call 'real bonds', which are described later.)

Equities (also described as shares or stocks)

This is one of the two fundamental investment types. When you buy a share or stock, you're buying ownership in a company. Through this ownership you are entitled to two things: a periodic dividend payment (generally paid annually, or for larger companies semi-annually) and participation in the increase or decrease in the overall value of the company.

Many people start by investing their money in these, because you can buy shares across a full price spectrum, from pence to thousands of pounds. Shares can be traded through an account you set up with a broker (which can be executed via the internet). If you're interested in investing in equities, consider diversifying your risk by investing through unit trusts, funds or collectives. These are managed by professional investment managers, whose investment materials will be given to you to review, so that you can see what they are investing in. Rather than buying shares yourself in individual companies, you'll be buying shares in pools of investment they manage – so you won't have all your financial eggs in one basket.

Bonds (debt)

Bonds are issued by a government or company to raise money. When you invest in these, you're investing in what is in effect an IOU from the issuer – basically, a kind of formal loan. The issuer commits to pay you interest at a specified rate on specified dates, and to pay the principal amount of the bond when it reaches maturity (the agreed end of the loan period). The rate of interest the borrower commits to paying depends on the perceived level of risk investors have of the borrower. If investors think the borrower is absolutely certain to make the payments as they fall due, the interest rate will be lower (because they are lower risk) than if they think the issuer is less likely to make the specified payments. Historically, bonds were issued in large denominations, tens of thousands of pounds, which made them inaccessible to the majority of private investors. The only way to invest in them was through unit trusts, funds or collectives that operate as described in the preceding paragraph. That changed in 2010 when the London Stock Exchange launched a retail bond platform, enabling direct access to this market, in addition to the previous ways.

General economic environment

This is a description of what is going on in the environment around you: what government is in power, what are UK interest rates doing, how are the EU and the euro doing, what is the rate of inflation, and so on. This overall environment will have a huge impact on your investments. I hear lots of complaints at the moment about the low returns on investments – 'What is the point of saving if I get so little interest?' Well, the flip side of earning a low interest rate on deposits is that the interest rate on any money you borrow will also be low.

TIP

Five UK personal finances podcasts every investor should download:

meaningfulmoney.tv;

financialwell-being.co.uk;

moneytothemasses.com;

thepropertyhub.net;

ukmoneybloggers.com/podcast/.

Savings accounts

For most people, the savings starting point is likely to be deposit/savings accounts at a bank or elsewhere. What you're aiming for is to: ensure your money is safe, be able to get to it when you need it within agreed time constraints, and get paid for letting someone else use your money.

Your bank

The easiest place to save money is with the bank where you have your current account. Setting up a savings account is as easy as filling in a form, because your bank knows who you are. You can set up a standing order with the bank, instructing them to move a specific amount of money from your current account to your deposit account on a regular basis. This self-inflicted savings plan was cited by several people as a good way to keep them from spending all the money they earned.

The downside of keeping your savings invested in a deposit account, whether it's at your current bank or another bank, is that the bank won't pay you much for leaving your money there. This is because the bank is low risk to you and you can get hold of your money at a moment's notice. The UK government guarantees that money on deposit at a bank will always be paid back to you, that is, returned to you even if the bank goes bankrupt, up to a total of £85,000. Keep in mind that the £85,000 protection covers all of your accounts at one bank. In other words, if you have both a current and a savings account with a bank, and their combined value is more than £85,000, not all of your money will be protected.

Interest earned

If you have £1,000 on deposit in a bank account all month and the AER is 1 per cent, you'll earn £0.83 interest in a month (£1,000 times 0.01 divided by 12). If you leave £1,000 in the account all year, you'll earn £10 interest if you're on an annual interest payment scheme, and about 0.05 per cent more if you're paid interest monthly. The latter is because you'll earn interest *on the interest* you have been paid, because that interest will be added to your account balance, as well as to the figure used to do the interest earned calculation (this is called '**compound interest**'). However, banks often offer a slightly lower rate of interest on monthly payment accounts, thus removing that advantage.

If you want to earn a higher interest rate but want to keep your money at a bank, you'll need to commit to leaving your money with the bank for a set period of time. The larger the amount you invest, and the longer it's tied up, the higher the rate of interest you'll earn. What you *don't* want to do is tie up so much money that when you need cash you either have to pay a penalty or borrow money elsewhere at a higher rate than what you're earning on the deposit.

Other banks

It is well worth looking at other banks to see what they are offering. There are online firms like moneysupermarket.com that provide product comparisons, and the money sections of the Sunday papers include lists of rates provided by many banks on many of their products. You'll find lists of 'the best' deals on offer at the moment on current accounts, savings accounts and other investments.

It pays to shop around, but don't get *too* clever, as the difference in what your money earns may not be worth your time or the hassle. Whether or not it is depends on two things – the amount of money you're looking to invest and the interest rate you can earn. Let's say you're planning to put £1,000 in a bank for a year and your bank offers you 1 per cent interest and another offers you 1.5 per cent interest. The difference in what you will earn (before tax) over that year is £5. Your bank will pay you £10 (£1,000 times 0.01) and another bank would pay you £15 (£1,000 times 0.015). You have to question whether it's worth your taking the time to open a new account. However, if the amount you put into the bank were £100,000, the difference would be £500, so it would probably be worth it.

National Savings and Investments

National Savings and Investments (NS&I) offers most, if not all, of the same savings/investment opportunities as banks do. The difference is that *all* of your money held with NS&I is guaranteed by the UK government (NS&I is an Executive Agency of the Chancellor of the Exchequer), compared with only the first £85,000 that you have at a bank. You will find that, as the risk to you is lower, so too will be the reward. You'll find NS&I products listed alongside other investment providers in cost comparison websites and newspaper tables, so you can easily compare products.

Individual Savings Accounts (ISAs)

The easiest way to save money tax-free is via an ISA, through which you can invest in a variety of assets. Any money you invest in these is tax-free – you pay no tax on any earnings or capital gains. If you have any savings at all that you don't think you will need in the near term, then putting it into an ISA is almost a no-brainer. With a cash ISA, there is no risk of the value decreasing – but the interest rate will be fairly low. For other ISA types, there is more upside and more risk. The key is to shop around.

Key ISA facts

- You can put money in an ISA account of your choosing and invest in a wide range of ISAs – cash, stocks and shares ('equities'), innovative finance (peer-to-peer lending and crowdfunding of debt instruments), Help to Buy or a Lifetime ISA.

- The government introduced ISAs in 1999 to encourage people to save money.

- You can invest up to £20,000 in ISAs during the 2019/20 tax year in almost any combination, with a few restrictions. There are limits on the Lifetime ISA and the Help to Buy ISA.

- If you don't invest the full allowance in a given year, you cannot carry forward the unused portion and invest more in a subsequent tax year.

- You are allowed to take money out of your ISA and put it back in during the tax year, but the total amount invested in the end must remain within the £20,000 ISA allowance.

- Check to make sure you're investing in a 'flexible' ISA, which means you can move your money in/out of ISA investment accounts.

- It's easy to see on the internet and in newspapers how various ISAs are performing, so do keep an eye on what you're earning. Don't hesitate to switch if you aren't satisfied with what you are earning.

- In the 2016/17 Budget, the government announced the Help to Buy ISA. This enables you to invest up to £1,200 in the first month and £200 in subsequent months in a designated ISA and, when you withdraw your money to purchase a home, the government will give you an additional 25 per cent of what you have on account. The amount is capped at £3,000, or 25 per cent of savings of £12,000. You must be a first-time buyer and purchase a property before 2030. The property value must be less than £450,000 in London and £250,000 outside London.

- The Lifetime ISA was launched on 6 April 2017. It enables those over the age of 18 to put £4,000 per year in an ISA and receive a 25 per cent bonus tax-free at the end of the year. From the 2018 tax year, investors received the bonus monthly.

- Many companies offer ISAs – banks, insurance companies, investment firms. If your ISA is with a bank, it's included in the UK government guarantee scheme mentioned earlier.

Cash ISAs

As mentioned in the box, plenty of firms offer these. In a nutshell, you deposit cash and you get interest at a rate consistent with the advertised AER on specified dates. You can arrange for that interest to be added to the ISA or paid out to you. It may not feel like a ton of money to you, or it may, but it is a start, and you'll get a higher rate of interest than you would get from a bank savings account (currently around 2.5 per cent to 3 per cent compared with 0 per cent on a basic bank savings account). Some cash ISAs have a minimum investment amount, and the higher that amount, the higher the rate of interest you'll get paid.

Stocks/shares/equity ISAs

There are two basic ways to invest in equity ISAs. The first is to invest in individual companies through a self-select ISA, which is usually managed by a stockbroker that you choose. The other is to invest through collective funds such as unit and investment trusts. As mentioned before, these are pooled investments managed by an investment manager who will spread the investment risk across a range of individual companies or industry groups.

The second approach is more commonly used, and if you decide to invest in share ISAs you'll find a wide variety of fund managers and funds to choose from. The returns on these ISAs are not certain like they are with cash ISAs. With these ISAs, you're hoping for increases in the value of the underlying shares or fund, and that the overall return will therefore be greater than what you would earn on a cash ISA. And your hopes may well materialize! But you have to remember that the value of what you invest in *may or may not* increase in value.

Any decision to invest in stocks and shares is a complicated one, and this is no exception. There are complications around what is tax-effective, and for some of these ISAs there are only tax benefits to higher-rate taxpayers. Therefore, when you consider these, make sure you read the materials carefully. When you make an investment in a share ISA, you'll do it through a third-party adviser who will charge you a fee for making the arrangements for you.

Other investment opportunities

When you consider how you move up the money ladder it can go a bit like this: meet your basic needs like housing, food, socializing; then start saving a bit, maybe in an ISA or company pension; then you invest in a home or have some other big event like having children (which costs lots of money!). And then, when all those needs are met, you may have money left over. If you do, or if you don't want to wait that long but are interested in investing your money, hoping to make it grow faster than it would otherwise, there are lots of different types of investment opportunities.

Two things that I have learned from experience are: you *must have a strategy* around what you're doing – indiscriminately investing in stuff that catches your eye is random! You may as well buy lottery tickets. You also need to think long-term; don't expect to turn a quick profit.

I want to be very clear that I am not giving you advice – the intention here is to expose you to some ideas that you may want to explore further. There are whole books written about investments. Let's take a look at some of the more typical investment opportunities that you may come across at your stage of life.

National Savings and Investment Premium Bonds

As mentioned earlier, you can buy financial products from the NS&I, which operates under the Chancellor of the Exchequer. Anyone over the age of 16 can invest a minimum of £25 and a maximum of £50,000. You won't receive interest on your investment, but you'll be included in a monthly draw for prize money. Those prizes can be up to £1 million and all winnings are tax-free. The minimum prize awarded is £25 and you have a one in 24,500 chance of winning a prize in the monthly draw. The chance of winning £1 million is 39 billion to one. Any money you invest is 100 per cent guaranteed by the UK government and you can take your money out whenever you want. The total pool of prize money is set based on the relative risk of the investment. Since it's government guaranteed, it's pretty low. As of June 2018, the annual prize rate is 1.4 per cent.

Equities (shares, stocks)

Equities are described earlier in this chapter so I won't repeat the information. However, I do want to mention again that it is likely that you will want to invest through *collective unit trusts* to spread your investment risk more broadly than if you picked individual shares. Those trusts may invest in shares listed on the London Stock Exchange or AIM (the Alternative Investment Market). The former has all the major companies listed, and AIM is for start-ups that are big enough for people to be interested in buying shares in.

If you're thinking about getting directly involved in the equity markets, be aware that buying and selling shares sounds easy, but making money is *not*. To get involved, you'll need to get an account through a stockbroker/adviser. It's easy to set up, and once it is, you can do all your buying and selling online. The broker will charge you a fee for each trade, so you need to factor that into your financial planning. On the other hand, if you want someone to advise you on what to buy and sell, you can hire a financial adviser to do so.

If you sell a share for more than it originally cost you, you will have a **capital gain**. Capital gains currently attract tax at a lower rate than income does. If you lose money you'll have a **capital loss** that you may be able to offset against future gains. You need to keep good records of your investment activities to help you complete your annual tax return.

Bonds (debt)

We looked at these earlier in the chapter; when you invest in a bond, you're buying the debt of an entity or government. Like equities, the value can go *up or down* based upon the market perception of the risk that the issuer will be unable to pay the interest payments or principal when it's supposed to. The price of the bond at any given time will take into account (sort of compensate for) the two fixed payment commitments of principal and interest rate and what that means for the investor at a given point in time.

An example: say the bond you're buying has a stated interest rate of 5 per cent, but the current rate of interest the issuer would incur if it borrowed new money is 2 per cent. In order to make up for that disparity in rates, the bond will be traded above the principal amount. That means that over the course of the bond's existence, its purchase and sale price may go up and down based on interest rates and market sentiment. However, at maturity, whoever holds the bond gets the full amount of principal. This can be a bit confusing, so if you want to invest in this way you do need to take the time to understand it. (You can read more about potential investments which will make this all clearer at the-right-side.co.uk.) Many corporate bonds are traded on the London Stock Exchange. Many investors choose to invest in these bonds via funds and collective trusts, managed by experienced fund managers who diversify risk by investing across a range of bonds.

You can also invest in UK gilts; by doing so you're lending money to the UK government. These are issued and traded in denominations of £100, and can be traded in lots of any size, which makes them an appealing place to start if you want to try out bonds. If you want to invest in gilts you'll need to go through a broker, just like with shares. You may also be able to invest in new gilt issues, which are often sold directly to the public at dates disclosed at the Debt Management Office website (dmo.gov.uk).

Commodities

Investing in commodities is the same as investing in stocks and bonds, but what you or a fund manager is doing is investing in *goods* rather than companies (things like coffee, gold, silver, pork bellies and oil). It isn't possible to buy and sell the majority of commodities directly as an individual, so you have to do it via a broker, although this is changing with the increased interest in commodities such as gold and silver. A few firms have been established to facilitate individuals who are interested in dealing directly in commodities, for example www.therealasset.co.uk. You're also able to buy gold from a machine at the Westfield shopping centre in London, with more dispensers planned in other locations!

Cryptocurrencies

You may have read about cryptocurrencies in the past few years. They are virtual currencies, with the best known being Bitcoin. There are many others, though, such as Ethereum, Ripple, Litecoin and so on. The value of these, unlike real currencies like the pound or dollar, fluctuates based on what the market perceives as their value. You may have read of many people making a great deal of money when the value of one Bitcoin went from $2,000 to $20,000 in the space of a year. But what goes up comes down: as Bitcoin did. You can invest in these by opening an account at selected brokers (like Plus500) or cryptocurrency 'wallet' providers; but please recognize that this is a high-risk investment.

Start-up companies

The UK government encourages people to start businesses and provides tax incentives for doing so. You may at some point be given the chance to invest directly in businesses being set up by friends, relatives or business colleagues. You can also invest in starts-ups via crowdfunding websites such as Crowdcube, Kickstarter and SyndicateRoom. These investment firms are under review by the UK regulators, as there have been several cases of the investments going bankrupt, so be careful.

Start-up successes

Bill Gates of Microsoft made a lot of his friends, family members and early employees rich by letting them invest in, and giving them shares in, his fledgling company. You may also have read the story about the guy who painted the mural in Facebook's offices and was paid in shares, which turned out to be a good rate of pay!

Your own business

You may be thinking of starting your own business, either on a part-time or full-time basis. If you do, be aware that the government provides substantial tax incentives to investors under the Seed Enterprise Investment Scheme and the Enterprise Investment Scheme. Banks, local authorities and other organizations provide many types of advisory and financial information for new businesses – so take full advantage of them.

We all seem to think that a new business has to be a totally new and radical concept. I hear people say, 'I can't think of something new' or 'If I had a new product/idea I would start a business'. Having a big idea is one way to start a business, but there are plenty of successful companies that didn't develop something totally new, instead delivering a product or service just a little bit better, faster or cheaper than an existing business. And some just executed their strategy better or had more effective marketing than the next guy.

Do keep in mind that once you set up a company, you will have to file an annual company tax return.

Property

When you mention investments, people frequently cite property. They some-times lose sight of whether the place they live in is an investment or a home! It only really counts as an investment if you are willing to convert it into cash – which many people aren't willing to do with their homes. As men-tioned earlier, houses aren't liquid assets, so even if you want to convert your home to cash, you may not be able to at the moment you want or need to.

Over the past 50 years, home ownership has been a good way to make money in many regions of the UK. A lot of people I know bought houses that were a mess, lived in them, did lots of work themselves to make them better, and then sold them at a profit. That profit from buying and selling their home was tax-free (gains on primary residences aren't taxed) so, in some cases, they were able to make more money from doing up their homes than they did from their jobs.

In Chapter 9 we'll cover all aspects of buying property. I only mention it briefly here, as for some of you it might be an investment option you want to consider.

There are two potential property investments to mention: first, buy-to-let investments, where you purchase a property solely to rent it out. The inten-tion is to at least break even on an ongoing-cost basis and to benefit from later capital appreciation. As you know, there are a few risks inherent in that idea. In the past few years, the government has imposed regulations which limit the interest deductions that owners can take and have increased the capital gains taxes on these investments, making them far less attractive in-vestments. Bear in mind, too, that buy-to-let mortgage rates are higher than rates for your primary residence. There are plenty of books covering this topic, so if you're interested in pursuing this investment idea, get hold of one. Second, commercial property (offices and shops rather than living accommodation) is an area of increasing investor interest. Direct investment by individuals is difficult because of the large sums of money involved, but you can now invest through property funds (along the same lines as you can invest in equities and bonds). They are increasing in popularity due to a perception that demand for commercial space will outstrip supply, which in turn will send rental and purchase prices up. But once again, there are significant risks inherent in this business model, not least of which is the amount of capital needed to buy big buildings.

Pensions – preparing for retirement

You may be wondering why you need to even think about retirement as you are just starting out in your career. The reason is that just like other savings, pension pots grow if you make little contributions often. Starting early also makes sense, because it gives you a longer period to have your pension funds grow, which means you can opt for riskier investments which are likely to provide higher returns in the long run.

So what is retirement? 'Back in the day', people worked at a set job, usually for their entire working life, and then they stopped working. Generally, people stopped at the age of 65 and collected money from the government (State Pension) and the employer's pension scheme (typically a defined benefit scheme where you were guaranteed a fixed salary from retirement till death). And those combined were sufficient to live on.

That scenario has changed significantly for several reasons. First, people are changing jobs more often than ever before, so they aren't creating big pension pots at their employer. Second, employers are no longer providing pension plans that provide in effect a retirement salary. Instead they are providing defined contribution plans where you have a pool of money that your employer and you contribute to, which then gets invested, and which you access when you reach retirement age. Third, retirement age is uncertain, and becoming increasingly so. Many people work past the historic retirement age of 65, and that trend is expected to continue. People will have to keep working if they don't have enough pension money to live on. And finally, it's uncertain if the government-provided pension fund will have sufficient money to meet the needs of the increasing old-age population.

So the best thing you can do to prepare yourself for the long-distance future is to build your pension from an early age. Make your National

Insurance contributions, contribute to your pension via auto-enrolment if your employer does not have a pension plan, contribute as much as you can to your employers' pension plans, and track your pension monies – where they are and what they are invested in.

Did you know?

A hundred thousand people retiring this year will face a life of poverty: they will retire with no personal pension savings and 15 per cent will be relying solely on the state pension.

Employment-related pension plans

When you're talking to a potential employer about a job, you need to ask whether the company has a pension plan and, if so, how much the company will pay into the plan on your behalf and how much you'll be required to pay. If they don't have a pension plan, they will be required to contribute to, and collect contributions from you for, the automatic enrolment pension. Your employer will also be taking National Insurance deductions from your pay, which go towards funding the government-provided pension.

National Insurance contributions

The details of what is withheld from your pay are covered in Chapter 8. The current full pension payment to beneficiaries is £164 per week. To receive that amount you'll have had to work for a specified period of years. See www.gov.uk/state-pension.

Auto-enrolment pensions

The government has mandated that all companies automatically enrol employees in pension plans and make contributions to them/deduct money from employees' gross pay. Any company that does not have a pension plan is required to enrol its employees in a government-operated automatic enrolment pension plan.

Employees joining a company who are over the age of 22 and who earn in excess of £10,000 will be automatically enrolled. This means the company will make contributions on your behalf, it will take deductions from your pay for your contribution, and the government will contribute to your pension via tax relief. If you don't meet the requirements, you can ask to join the company scheme. You can opt out of the scheme, which will require you to take action. From 2019, your employer has to ensure that 8 per cent of your eligible earnings are contributed to the plan, and the employer must contribute at least 3 per cent of that.

You will get tax relief on the amounts you pay in, and the actual amounts paid are based on pay earned of between £6,032 and £46,350. For additional information, please refer to www.pensionadvisoryservice.co.uk.

Company-provided pension plans

Many companies, larger ones in particular, will have a company pension plan. They will make contributions to a plan on your behalf, and you will most likely be required to make a contribution as well. The company will collect all of the money contributed by the firm and its employees and put them in a pool. An investment company will be retained to manage the pension monies, and you'll most likely be given some investment fund options to choose from.

The prevailing view on investment choices, though you have to decide for yourself, is that riskier investments are more appropriate for younger people than they are for older people. Why? Because of the risk/return trade-off. If a high-risk investment loses money but you're young, there is time for the investment to recover its value before you need the money. Not quite the same if you're older and take a big risk!

Your employer's pension plan should provide you with periodic statements explaining how much money you and your employer have contributed and what the value of the fund is (increased or decreased based on the investment portfolio's performance).

If you change jobs, you can leave your pension pot with your ex-employer, transfer it to your new employer or invest it yourself through a SIPP (explained below).

Tax benefits of pension contributions

There are great benefits to making personal pension contributions. The tax benefit works like this: you pay income tax on your earnings *before* any pension contribution, but the pension provider claims tax back from the government at the basic rate of 20 per cent. In practice, this means that for every

£80 you pay in, you end up with £100 in your pension pot. If you pay tax at the higher (40 per cent) rate, you have to claim the difference through your tax return or by telephoning or writing to HMRC. If you're an additional-rate (45 per cent) taxpayer, you'll have to claim the difference through your tax return.

Did you know?

As a result of automatic enrolment, more than 80 per cent of people are making pension contributions. However, if they considered their retirement money needs, most people would recognize that they are not putting enough money aside.

Self-invested personal pensions

The final way you can establish a tax-effective pension plan is through a self-invested personal pension (SIPP). This is a personal pension plan, approved by the government, which allows you to invest your money on your own behalf and benefit from tax relief. The government will allow you to invest in a broad, but not unlimited, variety of assets. *Unlike* other pension types, *you* are the person making the investment decisions. *Like* other pension types, the assets need to be segregated and in long-term investments. I won't go into details here, as you'll need to review the HMRC guidelines in effect at the time of making any decision about taking this approach.

It's down to you

As you can see, once you're generating more money than you need to live on, you will have many choices about what to do with it. The most important thing is to start managing your money inflows and outflows so that you have some money left over regularly, and keep yourself from spending it on things you don't really need or want. Look at the fun you can have exploring how to save and what to invest in! Even saving leftover pound coins to spend on something big after your collection efforts can be gratifying. And do plan for your future and old age, despite how far away that feels right now!

07
Handling a money shortage

In the previous chapter you learned how to budget, which will help you manage your money. From earlier chapters, you will have learned more about your approach to earning and spending money, and perhaps made some adjustments to help you improve how you manage the money you have. Your budgeting tools will help you monitor and target money coming in and out, and hopefully you will find ways to save money.

Does all that mean you will never have a money shortfall? Well, that would be unrealistic. Chances are that there will be times when you will find yourself short of money – either you got in less, or you spent more, than you expected. It's difficult to keep the money incomings and outgoings perfectly balanced. A small shortfall here and there can be met by drawing money out of your savings account, using credit cards or accessing authorized over-drafts. But what if you find yourself really short for a month or two? What if you don't have any savings to rely on?

I have heard way too many stories from people who have, for a number of reasons, got themselves way into debt, and also what they did to get themselves out of it. These were people in their mid-to-late 20s who had fallen into big debts without realizing what they were doing. The debts crept up, slowly at first – and then they accelerated. Many had been offered, and took up the offers of, numerous credit cards with zero or low interest rates. The providers then started charging normal interest rates, and the monthly costs pushed them further and further into debt. This is what you want to avoid. Therefore, when you have a shortfall, you need to think about how to find the funds to cover it at the lowest cost to you.

The costs of borrowing from banks and other institutions (eg credit cards, store cards) are covered in Chapter 9 and big borrowing decisions are addressed in Chapter 10. In this chapter, we will focus on unintended and short-term money shortfalls.

Your money habits

The habits you establish now, around avoiding money shortfalls and handling them well, are an important component of your ability to manage your money the way you want. Some people suffer only temporary cash shortfalls. They are careful, sticking to budgets, putting money aside for later, so they can draw on their savings account if they need money. It is only in the past 15 years or so that credit cards, overdrafts and store cards have been so widely offered, even to those with relatively low incomes, like students. Before that, we all existed with cash and cheques. If we went overdrawn, the penalties were large, so we worked hard to avoid running short of money.

It's still possible to manage your money that way. While researching, I found that some young adults who were given credit by their banks hardly ever used it. On the other hand, some borrowed as much as they could, maxing out on overdrafts and cards. The latter group was sometimes surprised when they had to pay the money back plus interest. University students often get caught out, as banks will offer them free overdrafts that become interest-bearing once they graduate. Apparently, more than half of all UK university students do not understand that they will be charged interest on bank loans!

Here are a few questions to get you thinking about your view of managing cash flow and debt:

- How would you feel if you were getting further and further into debt?
- How would you know it was happening? Would it matter to you?
- Would it matter enough that you would want to do something about it, or is it something you'd think about 'later on', if it does happen?
- Would you have the discipline to change whatever behaviour was the cause of the growing debt?

If you are at university now, here are a few additional questions to consider. Do you have plans for paying off your student debt in total? Or to pay it monthly as a payroll deduction? Which option is economically better for you? What are you doing about that 'free' overdraft that won't be 'free' forever?

Student loans

Depending on when you graduate, think carefully before rushing to pay off your student loan, beyond what is mandatory. While the interest payable on a student loan will be 6.1 per cent (remember it starts getting added to your borrowed balance as soon as you get the money), it may be a lower-cost way of borrowing than other loans, such as credit cards (19 per cent). So don't pay off your student loan and then have a cash crunch that means you have to borrow money from somewhere else!

I'm not suggesting you should never borrow money – that would not be realistic – but I *am* suggesting that when you do borrow money, you think it through. Avoid getting in an upward debt cycle where you keep throwing money away on paying interest on debt. If you do get into a debt swirl, prioritize repaying your loans based on the ones that are most expensive.

Most importantly, as soon as you think you may have an issue, *deal with it*! It's not going to go away on its own!

Your money values matter

Earlier on, we touched on your experiences with money while growing up and the impact they may have on how you manage your money today. This concept also applies to your approach to debt. Families manage their debt levels in lots of different ways; very few live the 'cash only' way, though I do know some who do. Many live prudently – reasonable mortgages for their home, maybe a car loan and credit cards they pay off most of the time and that sort of thing. Others take more risks – big mortgages relative to home value, sizeable personal loans, carrying large credit and store card balances.

People don't set out to get into financial difficulties; it usually happens little by little. They spend assuming they will get pay increases. They sign up for several credit cards and use them, suddenly finding they cannot pay them off at the end of the month. Those debts get bigger as interest is added each month, so paying them off gets harder.

Take a moment to think about the finances in your family. In particular, think about their views on debt – how were overdrafts, loans from friends, credit card and store card debts viewed and managed? What impact do you think your family background has had on your approach to taking on and managing debt? Do you want to follow that approach or do something different?

'Short-term lender Peachy found that nearly 40 per cent of Britons run out of money before payday. Of the people who did have money left at the end of the month, 56 per cent put the money into savings, 11 per cent blew the lot on socializing, with the rest leaving it in their current account.'

Kantar Media

Where to go to borrow money

So, what do you do, or what *will* you do, when you run short of cash? Each option described in this chapter will vary in terms of your ability to access funds and what you'll be charged for those funds. The actual cost to you will be impacted by how much you need, how long you need it, and how risky the lender thinks you are (based on your credit score).

Before you proceed, you will need to have answers to four questions:

- How much do I need to borrow?
- How long do I need to borrow it for?
- How much will it cost me in total (what you borrow plus interest)?
- How and when will I be able to pay it back?

As with any decision, you need to identify options, evaluate the pros and cons of each and then make a choice. When you need to borrow money, a key question is who is willing to lend you money and whether they have it to lend you.

Here are places you can turn to when you need funds.

Family

There may be many reasons why this is not where you want to go when you need money. Perhaps you have already exhausted this option. Perhaps no one in your family has money to lend you, even if you were willing to ask. Maybe you don't want to ask your family because you don't want them to know you are in a muddle. But, if your shortage is legitimate and one-off and you think someone in your family has the money to lend you, it is worth starting there.

The most effective approach to a family member is a respectful one. Explain your situation, how it came about, and how you plan to work your way out of it. Offer to borrow money on commercial terms, paying a fair rate of interest and committing to a repayment date. Borrowing from a relative can be a win–win because if they have cash in the bank earning a low interest rate and you offer them a higher rate, which is still lower than you would have to pay elsewhere, you will both be happy.

Friends

For small, short-term needs this can be a good option. But as with family, agree a repayment date and stick to it!

It is easy to forget who lent what to whom, so, as soon as you lend or borrow money, write it down. And if, or as soon as, you find you can't make a payment, talk to your friend. Good friendships can go bad if the lender has to ask repeatedly for repayment. No one likes a friendship to be taken for granted in any way, let alone financially.

Banks

This is a natural place to turn, as they're in the business of lending money… though it may be that the lending they have provided is what landed you in trouble in the first place. (Chapter 9 includes a lot of information about banks and explains terminology used below, so flip to that chapter if anything is unclear.) Always remember that banks are in the business of making *money from you*. They will *always* charge more to lend you money than they will give you on money you have deposited with them. The short-term loans you get from the banks, through overdraft facilities and credit cards, may be free to you now, but they will not be free forever – so consider carefully how dependent you want to get on those.

If your bank account runs out of money and you have an arrangement in place that they will automatically lend you money ('authorized overdraft'), they will charge you for using their money. If you don't have an arrangement in place ('unauthorized overdraft'), they are also likely to lend you a bit of money – and will charge you more! Look now to see what arrangements you have and what the charges are; typically, a fixed fee and a charge per transaction. This is expensive borrowing. Most banks will now send you an automatic e-mail or text message when you are getting close to zero on your account – so take action!

If you do go overdrawn, check your bank statement carefully for how your cash receipts and payments were processed. Banks are now required to process all direct credits to your account (things that increase your balance, such as pay) before they process debits (payments out).

Don't draw the cash you need on your credit card, as it will be treated by the card provider as a loan at a very high rate of interest. If you're going to do this, read the terms and conditions for the credit card to make sure you understand the cost that you will incur.

Always read the fine print in the terms and conditions provided by a bank for any product. If something happens and you feel hard done by, do complain to the bank, clearly explaining the situation and suggesting how they could remedy your situation. This is typically done by calling a complaints number provided in the terms and conditions the bank gave you when you opened your account or set up your overdraft. Be aware that you will probably be ringing into a call centre, manned by people who handle frustrated customers all day, so make it easy for them to help you – be polite and assertive, rather than aggressive. If, after dealing with the bank, you're still not satisfied, you should contact the Financial Ombudsman Service via www.financial-ombudsman.org.uk.

Banks will also offer you loans for car purchases, personal finance needs and home purchases (mortgages). The amount they lend you, the length (term) of the loan and the interest rate will be impacted by the bank's perceived risk of lending you money. If you take out a bank loan and at some point during the term of the loan you find you are struggling to meet your payments, get in touch with the bank as soon as you see you have a potential problem. Don't think to yourself: 'Well, things will get better.' They usually *don't* get better without a change in your money management strategy, which may take a bit of time. If you talk with your bank early, the bank may let you have a payment holiday to give you time to sort yourself out.

It is a *huge* mistake to make a payment on a long-term loan, like a mortgage, with a credit card. Doing that will increase the speed with which your financial situation will deteriorate, because long-term borrowing rates are lower (call it 4 per cent) than short-term ones (currently around 19 per cent on bank credit cards). By paying your mortgage with the card, you are turn-ing the cost of borrowing money from 4 per cent to 19 per cent – obviously not a good thing to do.

The internet

If you need money quickly and for the short term you can turn to the internet. If you search on 'borrow money', 'payday lenders' or 'short-term money loans', a list of lenders will come up. Many of these lenders have closed down since the UK regulator put restrictions on their fee-charging arrangements. Their fees used to be unrestricted but, since late 2014, you can only be charged 0.8 per cent of the loan amount per day, £15 for defaulting on your loan and total costs of borrowing of 100 per cent of the original amount borrowed. There has been a great deal of press cov-erage about these lenders, most of it negative. However, if one is objective about the costs, these can be the most cost-effective way to borrow money. The *big* 'but' here is that whenever you borrow money, you *must* know how and when you are going to repay it. Take a look at moneysupermarket.com, as it has a cost comparison facility, and outlines the risks of these loans in great detail. You need to compare the actual money this will cost you versus a bank overdraft – and don't assume the bank is cheaper.

I know people who have successfully and unsuccessfully used some of these firms. It is always best to avoid having to borrow money, particularly at a high interest rate. If you must, make sure you are totally sure you will be able to pay it back on the initial day you agree to. Read the small print, particularly regarding repayment procedures, as they are very detailed and it is easy to trip up on them. Several people told me about the difficulties they had when they tried to pay back what they had borrowed.

What the payday loan firms are very good at is processing customer re-quests quickly, which adds to their risk of lending. They will turn loan ap-plications around in hours, not the days or weeks a bank may take. They will do a basic check of credit information, including your credit, employ-ment, and any borrowing repayment history. In effect, they do their own credit scoring to put you in a high-, medium- or low-risk category, which they then use to set the rate of interest they will charge you. If you do take this route, look carefully at the details provided on the website. And most importantly, make sure you are going to be able to pay the loan back at the end of the term.

Payday loan costs

Are payday loan providers really that expensive? Let's assume you borrow £200 from a high-street bank for a month under an unplanned overdraft arrangement. That £200 will cost you £80 in overdraft fees, not to mention any charges for returned items and interest on the outstanding balance. To borrow £200 from an average payday/short-term lender will cost you around £66.

Pawnbrokers

You can use these firms to raise money quickly. This is how it works: you take something valuable (this is a potential limitation; they only accept luxury items like expensive jewellery, watches and antiques) and they lend you money for a period of time, at a fraction of the value of what you leave with them. In the past you had to go to a shop, but now you can go online and post your goods to them. Using the shop online facility, you can find out how much the shop will lend you and at what rate before you send your goods to them. You will have to pay the loan back in regular instalments, as well as the related interest. If you pay the interest and loan in accordance with your agreement, you get your possession back. If you don't, they take possession of your valuable item. They in turn will sell that item to get their money back.

If you want to learn more, take a look at borro.com.

Unauthorized lenders

I mention these with some trepidation, as I don't want to give this group airtime, but you need to be aware of them. These are some not very nice people who take advantage of those in financial distress, those who are desperate for money and can't get it anywhere else. The reasons may include, among other things, being an illegal immigrant; having no credit rating; not knowing how banks or other means of fund-raising work; and being illiterate. When people *need* money, say to put food on the table for their children, they will turn wherever they have to. Unauthorized lenders (sometimes referred to as loan sharks) provide money at *huge* interest rates and, if they aren't paid, the situation can deteriorate to one of physical danger. **Avoid these at all costs.**

Getting into and staying out of a mess

Whatever approach you take to borrowing money to get you through a short-term challenge (a gentle reminder that if you manage your money effectively, this will be a one-off short-term blip), you will need to find a way to pay the interest and loan back. Revisiting your budget will help you sort this out in the longer term, but when you're in a jam, make a fast decision and cut your spending to the absolute bare minimum.

Go back and review your budgeting to figure out what went wrong. Was it on the money coming in side (for example, you couldn't work as much as you expected, your student loan money didn't come through), or did you overspend on usual stuff, or did you overspend on an unexpected outgoing like a holiday or car repairs?

Go back and budget again, including planning for those one-offs. Remember that to keep in control a good money goal is to have enough savings in place to cover your costs for six months. To figure out ways to do that, take a look at Chapter 5.

A learning opportunity

Don't sweat the one-off money lapses. The key is to learn to see them early, and recover quickly. Recovery is manageable as long as the money hole is not too big and it hasn't existed for long, so watch your money carefully throughout the month and during your monthly budget review.

One of the best techniques to help you stay within your spending budget is to slow down your spending decisions. Stop to think:

- Do I really want that?
- Do I really need that?
- Is it worth going off budget or overdrawn for?
- How will I feel about this tomorrow?
- Whatever it is, can I get it cheaper?

There will be times in your life when you decide to take a big leap financially, like when you buy a car or a home, go on a long blow-out holiday or give up your job because you hate it. These may be life-defining moments in many ways. They can turn out to be some of the greatest life and money opportunities, despite what they feel like at the time. The work you're doing *now* to manage your money, learn about financial options and save a bit will all serve you well. Yes, even digging yourself out of a self-inflicted money black hole is going to be useful. So go easy on yourself, get sorted and move on.

Some money learning opportunities are missed out on due to well-intentioned parents. It can seem easy for parents, if they have the money, to bail their offspring out of financial problems. I know parents who are always there to top up allowance overspends, provide cars and insurance, and provide housing. As a result, their children don't learn about managing their money, which always ends in tears! So, tempting as it might be, don't let your parents do this to you.

Learning and practising *now* to set and remain within budgets, as well as learning about borrowing, will save you lots of headaches in the future – I promise!

08
Financial basics

Pay related

The next two chapters provide basic information about financial things you need to know about. They're designed for you to take a quick read-through, to gain a general awareness of what to look out for. Then, when the need arises, you can dip back into the relevant pages. This chapter covers all things pay related and the next chapter covers everything else. The tax authority rates for 2019/2020 are reflected here (note that Scottish taxpayers pay an additional 1 per cent tax on these rates). For subsequent years, please check hmrc.gov.uk.

I have yet to meet a person who is not surprised when they receive their first payslip. You may have agreed an hourly pay rate, expecting to take home that rate times the number of hours worked, or you may have agreed an annual salary, expecting to take home a twelfth of that amount at the end of the month. And then, what comes into your bank account? A much smaller amount!

This chapter assumes you are employed by a company (you could be a sole trader or working for a partnership). That company is required by law to process your pay through a payroll system, and ensure that amounts required by the government, and as set out in your employment contract (pension, benefits and so on), are withheld from your pay to be passed on to the relevant parties.

Of course, your employer may not process your pay through a payroll system. You could be paid 'cash in hand', which is your hourly rate times hours worked, with no deductions. This is most likely if you are doing short-term casual work, like painting a family friend's house or doing garden work over the summer. Or you could be paid partially through a payroll system and partially as cash in hand. This mixed arrangement is common where your pay includes a wage and tips, for example working in a pub. Be aware that under UK tax law you are responsible for taking all cash-in-hand pay into account when you figure out if you need to pay UK income tax. It is important that you keep a good record of the cash you have received, from whom and when, so that you can decide if you need to file a tax return. We'll come back to that later.

Your payslip

While you were in the process of being hired, you should have been told how often you'll be paid. If not, ask now, as knowing how often and when you're being paid matters for your money management! The money you earn will most likely be paid directly into your bank account. For all jobs, you will do the work before you get paid – this is called being 'paid in arrears'. That means that if you are on a monthly payroll cycle (usually payments are made some time after the 20th of the month), and you start work on the first of the month, you will have to wait some time to get any money. The same is true if you are on a weekly payroll, but the wait is obviously shorter.

When you're paid, your employer will give you, or give you access via a website to, a payslip. This includes important information, and keeping a copy in a file somewhere is a good idea Your payslip will look similar to the one in Figure 8.1, and an explanation of what you will see and the terminology used is detailed below.

Gross pay

This is the total amount of money you earned for the pay period. It will be based on your annual salary or your hourly rate. If you're paid an hourly rate, it will be the hours worked multiplied by the rate. If your employment agreement includes extra pay for working long or unsociable hours, that should also be reflected, so check the figures carefully. If you're on an annual salary and are paid monthly, your gross pay will be 1/12th of the annual salary amount.

Income tax withheld under the Pay As You Earn (PAYE) obligations

Your employer is required to collect money on behalf of HMRC for income taxes each time you are paid. The amount withheld from your pay cheque is mandated by HMRC, based on how much money you are likely to earn

Figure 8.1   Example payslip

Ref.	Employee Name				Process Date	N.I. Number	
139	A. N. Onymous				30-06-2019	AB123456C	

Payments	Units	Rate	Amount	Deductions	Amount
Salary	1.00	1500.00	1500.00	PAYE Tax	91.67
				National Insurance	77.68
				Student Loan	0.00
				Pension	12.00
				London Travelcard Loan	133.33

An Employer Ltd		This Period		Year To date	
		Total Gross Pay	1500.00	Total Gross Pay TD	4500.00
Tax Period:	3	Gross for Tax	1500.00	Gross for Tax TD	4500.00
		Tax Paid	91.67	Tax Paid TD	275.01
Tax Code:	1250L	Earnings for NI	1499.00	Earnings for NI TD	4498.00
Department:	1	National Insurance	77.68	National Insurance TD	233.04
		Pension (Inc AVC & APC)	12.00	Pension TD (Inc AVC)	36.00
Payment Method:	BACS	Employer NI	142.50	Employer NI TD	427.50
Payment Period:	Monthly	Employer Pension (Inc APC)	60.00	Employer Pension TD	180.00
				Employee APC TD	0.00
				Employer APC TD	0.00

	Net Pay	1185.32

during the current tax year. Later in this chapter we will cover how HMRC sets the withholding amount and how income tax is calculated, but for now, be aware that no tax is due on the first £12,500 you earn in the 2019/20 tax year (your 'personal allowance') and that rates applied to what you earn can vary from 0 to 45 per cent.

National Insurance (NI)

Your employer is required to deduct a percentage of your gross pay and send it to the government in the form of National Insurance (NI) contributions. These monies are used by the government to provide benefits such as retirement payments (pensions) and health services. The amount of NI withheld is reviewed annually in the Chancellor of the Exchequer's Budget. For the 2019/20 tax year, if you earn between £166 and £962 a week, you will have 12 per cent of your gross pay withheld on any earnings between those amounts. If you earn more than £962 per week, an additional 2 per cent will be withheld on earnings above £962. If you earn less than £162 in gross pay per week, no money will be withheld. (Your employer is also required to make NI contributions on your behalf, separate from what you pay. This has no impact on your payslip, but it's good to know.) One last thing before we leave NI – you should have received an NI number on a plastic card when you turned 16. If you didn't receive one, you will need to get one in order for your employer to pay you. To ensure you get the right benefits in the long term, you need to make sure that all of your pay and NI contributions are properly recorded in the NI system. To learn more about the UK NI system, search online for 'UKNI' – this will take you to the right place in the hmrc.gov.uk website.

Pension contributions

Pensions are covered more fully in Chapter 6. Your employment contract will set out whether your firm has its own pension plan, what contributions you will make (there may be mandatory and optional amounts) and what contributions your employer will make to the plan. If your firm does not have its own pension plan, you earn more than £10,000 a year and you're over the age of 22, you will be automatically enrolled in a government pension, requiring you and your employer to make contributions. Your contributions to whichever pension plan you are part of will appear as deductions from your gross pay.

Other deductions

There are other amounts that may be deducted from your gross pay, all of which should have been disclosed in your employment contract. What might these deductions be? Reimbursement for the cost of a uniform or work tools, charitable contributions you elected to make through a Give As You Earn (GAYE) scheme, private pension contributions, insurance payments or loan repayments, such as an annual travelcard loan. (The private pension contribution is described in Chapter 6.) Your employer may also be providing you with other benefits, which may be provided for 'free' or which you choose to purchase, like medical insurance, which will not appear on your payslip but will be included in your taxable income as described later.

Student loan deductions

If you have taken out a student loan and are earning income of a certain level, you will have deductions made from your gross pay to repay your student loan. You agreed to these terms when you originally signed up for the loan. How this works is explained more fully in Chapter 10.

Net pay

This is the amount of money that you will *actually get*, either deposited into your bank account or given to you in cash. This is your gross pay minus all agreed deductions.

Income tax

Once you start earning money, you need to consider income tax. There are many resources you can access to explain income and other tax (eg capital gains tax, value added tax), so I'm only going to cover the basics here, to ensure you're aware of the impact on the income you earn from work. The hmrc.gov.uk tax website provides very clear explanations, and there is a helpline to call if you want to talk to someone.

If you earn more money than the personal allowance (£12,500 for the 2019/20 tax year), then you will have to pay income taxes, and you may have to file a tax return. If your employer has withheld the correct amount of tax from your gross pay, you shouldn't need to file a tax return or do anything else. If HMRC thinks you owe money, they will send you a letter instructing you to file a tax return. Be aware that sometimes they do get it wrong; at the end of each tax year, it's a good idea to check your earnings and tax paid to see if you think you need to do anything more.

Your tax return must be filed with HMRC by the end of the January after the tax year end. (For example, for the tax year ended 5 April 2019 a tax return has to be filed by 31 January 2020.) If, however, you are filing on paper rather than online, and want HMRC to calculate your tax for you, this must be done by the **October** after the tax year ends (so, for the tax year ending April 2019, you must file by October 2019). If you don't meet those deadlines you will be fined – starting at £100 plus interest on the unpaid tax amount due. If you are more than three months late, the penalties will be even greater.

If you work for several employers, you need to add up what you received from all of them to come up with your *total earnings* when working out if you owe tax. If you move between companies, the tax forms you provide to each new company should ensure you have paid sufficient tax. But again, it is best to check this yourself.

The amount withheld from your pay cheque is supposed to approximate what you will owe the government by the end of the tax year, but for several reasons the amount withheld may not be the amount you actually need to pay. Because it doesn't always work out quite right, you need to do a calculation at the end of the tax year to figure out if you are owed money by, or you owe money to, the tax authorities. There are forms you will need to complete and submit to HMRC if you are in either situation.

Taxes for summer jobs

You don't always have to wait until the end of a tax year to ask for money owed to you. If you worked over the summer and won't be working for the remainder of the tax year, and you have overpaid tax, you can claim it back at the end of your summer job. (How to do this will be explained later, as well as what you can do to avoid that situation.)

Taxes if you are paid cash

Even if you are paid cash in hand, you need to think about taxes; being paid that way does not mean you don't have to pay tax. If you're being paid cash, it's a good idea to put 20 per cent of what you earn above £12,500 in a bank account or elsewhere where you will not be tempted to spend it, until you figure out if you owe tax money at the end of the tax year. And if you don't end up needing it – you will have a good amount of money to put into a savings account!

How to check that you're not paying too much tax. If tax is taken directly out of your income via PAYE, you should receive a tax code from HMRC once a year. The code will have numbers which indicate your tax-free allowance with a zero knocked off. The letter that follows represents your tax situation – see gov.uk/tax-codes. The most common is L. Check that your interest and dividend income is taxed correctly.

Money Week

Important tax facts

The UK tax year

The tax year runs from 6 April of one year to 5 April of the subsequent year. This means that you need to take the pay you earned between those two dates into account when figuring out the income you earned, the tax you paid and any under- or over-payment of tax.

Personal allowance

As described above, you can earn money up to this amount in a given tax year and not have to pay any income tax on it. For the 2019/20 UK tax year, the amount is £12,500. Be aware: this doesn't mean that income tax won't have been deducted under PAYE, so you need to check your payslips to make sure nothing has been withheld. If tax has been withheld, contact HMRC quickly to get it sorted.

Earned income versus taxable income

Earned income is another name for your gross pay, including any cash-in-hand amounts, earned during the tax year. Taxable income is the number you get when you subtract your personal allowance from your earned income.

Income tax rates

These are the percentage rates of income tax you will be required to pay on different levels of taxable income. These rates are reviewed annually on Budget Day and are easy to find on the internet (hmrc.gov.uk). For the 2019/20 UK tax year, the personal allowance is £12,500, which means that until your **earned income** is greater than that amount, you will have zero taxable income and, therefore, have no income tax obligation. Once you earn more than £12,500, you will have to pay tax. For earned income between £12,501 and £50,000, you will have to pay 20 per cent of what you earn, for amounts above £50,001 and below £150,000 you will have to pay 40 per cent tax and, for earnings above £150,001, you will have to pay 45 per cent tax. These three rates are called the 'basic' rate (20 per cent), the 'higher' rate (40 per cent) and the 'additional' rate (45 per cent). Note: if you are a Scottish taxpayer, each of those figures needs to be increased by 1 per cent – that is, 21 per cent, 41 per cent and 46 per cent for 'basic', 'higher' and 'additional' rates.

Table 8.1 lists a few examples of tax you would pay based on earned and taxable income, assuming you are a UK taxpayer.

Visit www.thesalarycalculator.co.uk to get an instant calculation of what your take-home pay should be.

Your tax code

This relatively simple concept tends to get complicated in practice, particularly in your early years of work. The purpose of the HMRC-provided tax code is to tell employers the amount of tax to deduct from your gross pay to derive your taxable income. The resulting taxable income is then subjected to the tax rates for each income band by your employer, who figures out how much tax to withhold from you and pay to HMRC. If the tax code is the right amount and all of your earnings go through a payroll system, you should not have to file a tax return.

Table 8.1   Tax payments example

Gross Income	Taxable Income	Tax Due	Effective Tax Rate	Explanation
£6,000	£0	£0	0%	The money is all yours, no income tax is due, because you earned less than your personal allowance.
£14,000	£1,500	£300	2.1%	Your taxable income is £14,000 minus £12,500 for your personal allowance, ie £1,500. Your tax due is £1,500 multiplied by 20%.
£55,000	£42,500	£9,500	17.3%	Your taxable income is £50,000 minus £12,500 for your personal allowance, ie £42,500. Of that, £37,500 is taxed at 20% (£7,500), and the balance, £5,000, is taxed at 40% (£2,000). That makes a total tax payable of £9,500.

The tax code will be numbers followed by one or two letters, the meaning of which is explained on the HMRC website. You should receive a letter from HMRC with your code and your employer will receive it as well. When you receive it, or when you get your first payslip, go to the HMRC website and figure out if the number makes sense. If it doesn't, speak to your employer and HMRC immediately.

When you first begin your permanent working career (ie start work after you finish education), chances are it will take a few pay cycles to get your tax code sorted out. That's for two reasons: one is that HMRC doesn't have much information about you, so can't be sure if you're entitled to a full personal allowance. The other is that you probably aren't starting work on the first day of the tax year, so the automated systems of prorating figures and treating amounts as cumulative don't work well. See the 'Expect issues' section below (p 107).

If you feel your tax code is incorrect, go to the HRMC website (hmrc.gov.uk), where there are instructions for what to do about that. HMRC reviews all tax codes at the end of each tax year and after tax returns are filed, which may lead to an adjustment of your code, so keep an eye on your payslip.

Other earnings-related taxes

Benefits in kind

Your employer may offer you 'free' benefits in addition to paying you a salary or hourly wage to work. These benefits could include things like medical insurance, life assurance or a company car, all of which will have been explained to you in your employment contract. You will have been given the choice of taking up those benefits or not. At the end of the day, though, they're not totally 'free', as HMRC requires you to pay tax on their value. The estimated value will be reported by your employer to HMRC and your tax code adjusted during the year to take them into account.

Shortly after the end of the tax year, your employer will give you a P11D form which details the benefits' value. Review it as soon as you receive it, making sure it is what you expected, and follow up with your employer if it isn't. If the P11D amount is the same as what was taken into account for your tax code, you don't need to do anything. However, if the amount is different from what you expected, you will either need to reflect it on your tax return, if you have to file one, or arrange for your tax code to be adjusted for the following year.

Income from savings and investments

This can become quite a complex area. The key concepts to know are:

- Income from savings and investments, ie dividends and interest, is taxed in the same way as earned income, which means it is subject to tax above specified amounts. There are specific rules which are explained in Chapter 6.

- Capital gains, which are gains from the purchase and subsequent sale of investment assets, are *not* taxed in the same way as earned income. Each individual is allowed to earn £12,000 (for 2019/20) of capital gains free of tax, and some asset sales (assets sold for less than £6,000, and your personal residence) are totally exempt from tax. The capital gains tax rate has, in recent history, been lower than income tax rates – 18 per cent of the gain for basic-rate taxpayers and 28 per cent for higher-rate taxpayers.

Communications with HMRC

There are numerous reasons why you may need to get in contact with HMRC and vice versa. A few things to bear in mind regarding those communications and related documentation are as follows.

Your tax office

You will be assigned a tax office that you're supposed to communicate with if you have any tax-related issues. It is determined by the physical location of your employer. You can call the office directly (make sure you get the name of the person you talk to). I highly recommend you always follow up any conversation with something in writing to avoid any misunderstanding and keep a copy of what you have written. If you can't figure out the tax office to contact, you can look it up on the HMRC website.

PAYE P45 form

When you stop working for a given employer, you should be given a P45 form. This informs you and HMRC of the income you have earned and income tax that has been withheld by that employer during the current tax year. Keep that document in a place where you can find it, as you will need it to review your situation at the end of the tax year. You will also need to give one sheet of it to your next employer.

PAYE P46 form

When you take on your first job, you won't have a P45 to give your employer, so you may be asked to complete a P46. This enables the employer and HMRC to calculate the right tax code.

PAYE P60 form

This is the form your existing employer will give you at the end of the tax year. You will need this form to figure out if you need to file a tax return and if you need to pay or reclaim income tax. The form provides details of earned income, income tax and National Insurance withheld and student loan deductions (if relevant). Armed with your P45 forms (previous employers) and P60 form (current employer) for the year, you will have all you need to figure out what your earnings and withholdings were.

Students working with no PAYE deduction/Form P38(S)

If you're a student and working during the school year or during the holidays, it may not be necessary for your employer to withhold income tax from you – as long as you won't be earning more than the personal allowance. To make this arrangement, you should print the P38(S) form from the HMRC website, complete it and give it to your employer. Do it as soon as you agree to do the job, so your employer can deal with it before processing your first payment. **Be aware** – I have not yet come across a single employer who knows about this or that it was possible, so *you* will need to drive the process.

Students working with PAYE deduction and later reclaim/Form P50

If you're a student working during the holidays or during a gap year and income tax *has* been withheld, you can reclaim this money by filing a tax return after the end of the tax year. Or you can send a letter to your tax office, including your P45 and P60 forms, explaining your situation. But the quickest way to get your money back, if you're not going to work for the remainder of the tax year because you are returning to your studies, is to complete a P50 and submit that to your tax office, keeping a copy of your form.

Getting money back from HMRC

If you believe that HMRC owes you money, you can either wait until the end of the tax year or request repayment earlier (only if you aren't going to earn any more money during the current tax year). The easiest way to figure out if you are owed money is on the HMRC website at www.thesalarycalculator. co.uk. The site gives clear instructions that take you through the process of filing a repayment request. Make sure you print out and save a copy of whatever you provide to HMRC.

A clear letter to HMRC will speed the process, so make sure you explain your situation fully, including: who you worked for; how much you earned; what you were paid; the fact you are not working again until whenever; and anything else that may help. Remember as you write your letter that the recipient knows nothing about you or your situation, so provide *all* of the information they might need. Make sure you include relevant source documents like P45s and P60s. Be polite and persevere, first via letters. If you've had a few goes and your money has not arrived, it's worth trying to call the person who wrote to you, as identified in the most recent letter, or call the general tax office number. As annoying as it may be to explain your story again and again, remain calm and try to ascertain what you can do to help them help you. Start by asking them what, if anything, is missing. Keep in mind that these situations always work out in the end!

Filing a tax return

At the end of the tax year, you need to collect all of your earnings information to determine if you need to file a tax return and/or are due to pay/ receive money to/from HMRC. If your income has all gone through PAYE, and the withheld amounts were correct, chances are you won't have to do anything. If you get income from other sources, chances are you *will* need to file a return. To confirm whether or not you must file a return, check on the HMRC website. I recommend you always do an income earned and tax paid calculation and keep a record of it, whether or not you have to file a return.

If you *do* need to file a return, you will probably be able to file it using the HMRC online system. This is well worth doing if HMRC owes you money, as it speeds up the repayment process. If you file the return as soon as the tax year is over rather than waiting until the filing deadline, you will get your money back sooner. If, on the other hand, *you* owe money, you may want to complete a paper return and file it on 31st January – the final return due date – so you pay the money due as late as possible. Remember, though: if you want HMRC to calculate how much tax you owe them, you must file before the previous October.

Expect issues

As I mentioned, when you are starting out in your career or working during summer or other holidays, it is best to expect a few issues. The reason is that HMRC's systems are set up to deal with ongoing wage (salary or hourly) earners. Here is a typical situation of what happens.

Assume you have a three-month summer job for which you will earn gross pay of £4,000. HMRC will provide a tax code and your employer will withhold from your gross pay the amount of tax you would have to pay if you worked and earned at the same rate *all year*. That means HMRC treats you as if you will earn £16,000 for the year (£4,000 times 4).

If your total earnings for a given tax year were £16,000, you would have to pay tax (for the amount you earned above the personal allowance), so withholding tax from your gross pay would be correct. But, if the only money you earned during the tax year was that £4,000, then you will not have to pay any tax at all on those earnings, so tax should not be withheld.

The HMRC website is very good at explaining anything to do with income taxes, and the search facility makes it easy to find what you're looking for.

There are three things I want to remind you to be diligent about:

- Figure out the amount of cash you will actually receive *before* you do your budgeting, as the impact of taxes could be significant.

- Check your first few payslips carefully – gross pay, net pay and tax code – and deal with any tax code issues as soon as possible.

- Keep your payslips in a binder, drawer or box, and keep good records, so that when you get to the end of the tax year it is easy for you to figure out what you earned, the cash you actually received, whether or not you need to file a tax return and whether you owe money to, or are owed money from, HMRC.

A few final words on taxes

This chapter should have helped you understand what impact income tax will have on your pay. It can be quite a shock to have what seems like so much money taken out of your pay. Your actual total tax rate includes not only income tax, but value added tax (VAT) at 20 per cent on most things you buy, other than food in shops, council tax, road tax and taxes on petrol, alcohol and cigarettes.

This seems a good place to address the frequently asked questions of: 'What can I do about it?' and 'How can I pay less tax?' The answer is 'not a lot', at least on your earned income. If you work in the UK, you have to pay UK income tax. The only real option is to move to another country. Once you leave the UK, you will not be subject to the UK tax regime... but you *will* be subject to the tax regime of the country you're living in. At the moment, there's quite a lot of movement of people east, where income taxes are lower (17 per cent in Hong Kong and 0 per cent in Dubai).

The only opportunities for a typical UK employee to reduce income taxes are in the areas of savings and pensions. The UK government is encouraging people to save and to make pension contributions, so there are tax incentives in these areas. These opportunities were described in Chapter 6, which you may want to reread now.

09
Financial basics
Everything else

In this chapter, we're going to go through key financial concepts and terms related to all things *except* your pay, focusing on those areas where I've most often seen people struggle or get into real difficulties. By the end of this chapter you will know:

- When you need a loan to buy a car, is an annual percentage rate (APR) of 10 per cent better or worse for you than an APR of 5 per cent?

- What is the difference between APR and annual equivalent rate (AER)? Big APR numbers are bad and big AER numbers are good – why is that?

- Why do you get 0 per cent interest if you leave your money in a current bank account? 1 per cent in a savings account? Or 3 per cent if you put it in a term deposit and commit to leaving it there for five years?

- What are the differences between a credit card, a debit card and a store card?

'Up to 8.8 million people are over-indebted. 13 million people do not have enough savings to support them for a month if they received a 25% cut in income. 50% of households in the bottom half of the income distribution do not have home contents insurance. Nearly 2 million adults do not have a bank account.'

2018 Financial Inclusion Commission report

The time value of money and the risk/reward trade-off principles

We touched on the three key financial principles early in the book. Two are highly relevant to what we'll cover in this chapter, so let's start with a brief reminder of those.

The time value of money principle describes the notion that money you have today is worth more to you than money you may receive in the future. A simple way to understand this is that if you have £100 and put it in your bank account on 1 January, you will earn interest on that money all year. By 31 December, what you have in your bank account will be more than £100 because of the interest you earn (say £105 if the bank interest rate is 5 per cent). However, if you received the £100 on 31 December, you'd obviously only have £100 on 31 December. Because of this principle, when you deposit money in a bank, or elsewhere, you expect to be paid interest on it; and when you are lent money, the lender expects you to *pay* interest.

Here's another example of the same principle: if you pay an entire year's car insurance premium up front, it will cost you less than if you pay it in 12 monthly instalments during the year. Why? Because the insurance company is better off if it receives its full year's money up front. This concept influences many aspects of finance.

The risk/reward trade-off principle describes the notion that the higher the risk you take, which means a higher risk of loss, the higher the potential reward should be. This is easy to explain using the UK National Lottery as an example. If you buy a ticket for £1, you could win millions, but the likelihood of that happening is tiny. In fact, statistically speaking, you're more likely to die of a heart attack before the prize is drawn than win the prize. Of course, by buying one ticket you haven't put much at risk. You could buy loads of tickets, which would increase your chance of winning... but you would have to buy an awful lot of tickets to increase your chance of winning significantly.

Compare that example with a £50 ticket you can buy at an airport to win a £100,000 car. Buying one of those tickets is pretty expensive, but, as there are not too many ticket holders, you have a better chance of winning than you do if you buy one lottery ticket – a better but still not great chance. In the second case you have more money at risk, a less valuable reward and a greater chance of winning. Sticking with the car example, if you bought all of the car tickets then you would win, but by then you probably would have paid more than the £100,000 the car would cost to buy outright. (What the raffle company is doing is betting they can get more money from tickets than the car cost them.)

The risk/reward principle explains why the amount of income you earn from lending or investing your money will depend on the level of risk you take. Similarly, the amount of money you are charged by a lender, and hence what the lender earns, will depend on the level of risk the lender thinks they are taking, that is, how risky you appear to be.

Bank accounts, debit cards, overdrafts and interest rates

The shape and form of 'retail' banking, which is the part of banking that provides services to you and me, has changed dramatically during the past 25 years. Back then there were no money machines, cheques were used extensively, credit cards were hardly used (John Lewis and Marks & Spencer would only allow you to use their store cards) and there was no internet, let alone internet banking. People actually went to their local bank and usually had a personal relationship with their local branch manager. The branch manager became a well-known person in the community, knowing everything about everyone and, as a result, was well positioned to decide if someone could afford a loan. It doesn't work that way anymore.

Historically, there were many banks to choose from, but over the past 20 years the industry has consolidated and the market is now dominated by the four big high-street banks (Lloyds, RBS, Barclays, HSBC), which serve more than 70 per cent of all consumers. The reason for the banking consolidation is the same as for other industries – scale matters for profitability.

The UK government and the Financial Conduct Authority, one of the banking regulators, have been facilitating the entry of banking start-ups, but progress in terms of taking market share from the big four has been limited. Chances are, your parents chose your bank and you're still using the same one. We each need to keep in mind that 'loyalty doesn't pay'; keep your eyes on the newspapers and internet (eg www.moneysavingexpert.co.uk) for the best deals on bank accounts, savings accounts, ISAs, insurance and everything else. It's now easy to move your account if you want to; banks are required by the regulator to effect an account transfer, including moving all of your direct debits and standing orders, within seven days.

Always remember that banks are in the business of *making money* from money. Most fundamentally, they take deposits from customers and pay them x per cent and lend the money out to others at x per cent plus y per cent. The objective is to pay as little money as they can *out* to customers for their deposits (keeping competition in mind), and charge *more* than that to customers for the loans provided to them. And what drives the interest rate the bank gives you for your deposit and charges you for a loan? The level of risk you take by depositing money with the bank, and the risk the bank takes by lending you money. The higher the risk, the higher the rate of interest. Banks argue that they are low risk, and therefore customers don't need to be paid much for the money held with them. Banks have processes for evaluating how risky you are and therefore how much they will lend you, and on what terms. For these arrangements to work, banks have to have the money back from the loans they have made, to give to the customers whose money is on deposit when they want to withdraw it.

Getting customers to deposit money is a key objective of banks, as those deposits enable the rest of a bank's business. Banks work hard at attracting customers from a young age. They start with young people's accounts that are opened jointly with their parents. That works well for the banks, as the parents will probably open the account at their own bank. Banks also work hard to attract college- and university-age clients, offering benefits to entice students to set up an account with them. You may be getting lots of approaches and will be hearing lots from your friends about good bank accounts. A number of incentives, such as free travel and iTunes cards, are being offered by banks. And they also offer 'free' overdrafts, which are covered in Chapter 7.

In short, deal with banks with your eyes open, always remembering they are in business to make money! Pay close attention to products and services your own bank offers and compare those with offerings from other banks. Banks are required to make this comparison easy. The number you need to know when you deposit money is the AER and when you borrow it is the APR. Both rates are driven by the base rate set by the Monetary Policy Committee of the Bank of England. The AER you earn reflects the risk of the institution holding your money and the length of time you give up control of your money, as those increase your risk. The APR you pay reflects the risk the institution is taking when it lends money to you. From your perspective, the bigger the AER and the smaller the APR the better. When you are borrowing money, you want a low APR, and when you are investing, you want a high AER.

AER and APR

Both AER and APR are expressed as percentages to make it easy to compare products. AER is the amount of interest income you earn on your deposit/investment for a year, divided by the amount of money you have deposited/invested. APR is the amount of interest you pay to borrow money for a year, divided by the amount of money borrowed.

A few people explained to me that they saw no benefit in saving money at the moment, as the AER on any savings is so low. Fair enough… but if interest rates on deposits increase, so too will interest rates on loans. Those two interest rate numbers are always correlated. Whatever the raw numbers, the banks will *always* charge customers more for their loans than they will pay customers for the money they have on deposit. That's the only way they can stay in business. It's the same when you change money into a different currency for holidays; the exchange rate board will show two prices – whether you are buying foreign currency or changing it back, you always get the worst price.

Let's look at more bank-related things.

Current account

The first bank account you open or probably will have opened by now will be a current account. Think of it as a wallet where you put money in and take money out on an ongoing basis. Money goes in, or is 'credited' to your account when you deposit cash or cheques, your parents put your allowance in, you receive a benefits payment or your employer transfers in your monthly/weekly pay. Money goes out, or is 'debited' from your account, when you withdraw money from a cash machine, use your debit card, or when money is withdrawn under a direct debit or standing order made by a vendor under your instructions. Every transaction will appear on your bank statement and will be reflected in your online information.

Direct debits and standing orders are automatic payments (usually monthly) taken out of your account. These are set up so you don't have to remember to send a cheque or instruct a payment every time a payment is due. You'll know that you have done this, because you will have signed a contract authorizing the payment. Examples of these could be your mobile phone bill, housing rental charges, university fees, council tax and utilities. The difference between these two is that under a standing order, the same amount goes out every time (think rent) and under a direct debit the amount will change based upon your usage (think phone contract). These debited amounts will appear on your bank statement.

Did you know?

A quarter of people under the age of 34 have never switched from their childhood bank accounts. More than half of 18- to 34-year-olds have not set foot in a bank in the past three months. More than a fifth have never deposited a cheque.

Daily Telegraph

Whenever you use your contactless debit card to make a payment, it will be going through this account. If you use a contactless debit or credit card, the amount charged will be listed on your bank or credit card statement (currently a £30 per transaction limit). If you are paying with a phone payment application, the funds will either be taken out of your bank account or applied to a credit card in line with what you requested when you set up the application.

While we rarely go into banks these days, the most likely reason you would go is to deposit money into your account. Having said that, some cash machines enable you to do this; and if it's a cheque you want to deposit, some banks allow you to send a photo of the cheque and they will add the funds to your account. If you do go into your bank, you will need to prepare a deposit slip and hand it, and the cheque/cash, to a cashier. The deposit slip just needs a date, the amount and a signature. You can also post cheques. If you do, check your account balance after a few days to make sure the cheque has been processed. If the funds don't turn up, you will have to notify whoever issued the cheque to cancel it and send a new one.

If you write a cheque, it will be drawn on your current account. To fill one in: date goes in the upper right; payee is the name of who you want to pay the money to (this needs to be the legal name of the payee or the bank will reject it – for example, my bank account is in my maiden name); amount to pay is included in figures on the right and must include two decimal points; amount to pay is written in words under the payee line. Make sure the numeric and word amounts are the same. Then sign it. All this may sound straightforward… but I have sent unsigned cheques, I have had cheques rejected due to writing the wrong name, and I have had cheques rejected for illegible or inconsistent amounts. Remember to write *all* of the relevant information on the slip in your cheque book.

As you can see, this bank account is an important one, as it holds a lot of information about what's going on with your cash; so keep a close eye on it. It's a good idea to check your account balance every time you go to a cash machine and to review at least monthly every transaction that has gone through it. With the new apps that are being offered around cash inflows and outflows, you can arrange to get a daily transaction listing, which I would encourage. (See Chapter 5 on budgeting.)

As you review your transactions, make sure you agree with every item that is listed as touching your account. As you do this, if you're using a money analysis app, you can also classify the expense into the category you want for your budgeting/analysis purposes. Any direct debits, standing orders and direct credits will have identifiers that tell you who originated the entry, which you should recognize. Cheques you've written will appear individually; if you deposit one cheque, the individual amount will be shown, but if you put a few cheques in as one deposit, only the total amount of the deposit will appear. If there's anything you don't recognize, get in touch with your bank immediately. Also consider if there is anything missing. In accordance with regulations, your bank has to reverse charges you think are incorrect, subject to investigation. This is described in the terms and conditions that you will have been given when you set up your account, which will also be available online. Read those carefully, as some banks now have exceptions. For example, if you have a weak password on your online account, your bank may refuse your claim.

One last thing to mention here is about the timing of money movements in and out of your account. Payments in and out of your bank account, except for cheques, are automatically processed via technology. In other words, when you tap your debit card to buy something, the money comes out of your account at that moment, as if you were taking cash out of your wallet. When you deposit a cheque, though, the money will not count as yours for several days, as the funds need to be cleared by the bank. 'Clearing' is the bank's process to make sure a cheque is legitimate, and that the cheque writer has the funds available in their account to pay over. It's during this process that a bank may find that the friend who gave you that cheque had no money in his account, so the cheque will be bounced. The same process happens when you write a cheque.

Your bank is required to 'give you credit' for any money that comes in during a day before it reflects the money outgoings. This is to reduce the amount of times people go overdrawn – which means you have run out of money and have a negative balance. See the 'Overdrafts' section below.

Packaged accounts

There are an increasing number of bank accounts and credit cards that offer you a package of services. For a monthly fee, you will have a normal current account but also receive perks, including cashback and shopping discounts. It's *critical* that you review the details of the offering very carefully, and evaluate whether the deal is a good one for you. An increasing number of complaints are being made about these accounts, which indicates to me that perhaps the perks weren't as valuable to customers as they thought they were going to be.

Debit cards

When you opened your current account, you will most likely have been given a debit card. It is called a debit card because each time you use it, the money is debited (ie removed) from your account, reducing the balance in the account. This is the card you use to get money out of cash machines and to pay for things in shops, restaurants and everywhere else. Any payments made with the card go out of your current bank account immediately and appear on your bank statement as of the date of the transaction. There is no charge for using the card. You need to keep close tabs on the current account the debit card is attached to, avoiding the possibility that you will spend more than the amount of money you have available in your account.

Free overdrafts, authorized overdrafts, unauthorized overdrafts and being overdrawn

You need to carefully monitor the amount of money that is in your current account. If the balance goes below zero, you are **overdrawn**. Banks offer overdrafts to some customers, which are like a safety net on your current account. Overdrafts allow you to automatically borrow up to a certain amount when there's no money in your account; they can be useful to cover short-term cash-flow problems, like if your rent goes out before you get paid, or if a bill is due before a cheque has cleared. You don't have to use it, but it's there if you need it.

Especially if you're a student, you may have a free overdraft, which means the bank won't charge you for borrowing that money; although you *do* have to pay the money back. If you don't have a free overdraft, you can ask your bank for an authorized overdraft. They'll decide whether to give you one based on your bank record, and you may have to pay a fee to set it up. You don't have to use this overdraft either. You will have to pay the overdraft back, plus interest plus a usage fee (typically £5). Read the overdraft terms and conditions carefully.

If you go overdrawn without your bank's authorization (this means below zero in your account if you don't have an approved overdraft, or go overdrawn by more than your 'approved overdraft' if you do have one), the bank calls this an unplanned/unauthorized overdraft. The charges for this kind of overdraft will be higher. It's common practice to charge a fee of £10 for *each day* that you are overdrawn, capped at around eight days. You will also be charged interest on the amount you have borrowed. Your bank may also refuse to pay on cheques you've written, or refuse to pay direct debits/ standing orders. You will be charged fees of around £10 for each refused transaction, in addition to the overdraft fees and charges. As you can see – this can very quickly add up! The UK regulators are putting pressure on banks to revisit these charges, as they make the cost of borrowing *very* expensive. If you annualized the cost, turning it into an APR, you would find that the rate is similar to, if not more than, what payday/short-term lenders charge.

If you're a student, you'll probably have been offered a free overdraft from your bank, or from other banks to attract you as a new customer. This is, in effect, a loan that won't cost you anything now. However, it may cost you in the future.

As your student days draw to a close, the bank(s) that have been providing you with an overdraft are likely to change the terms of your overdraft arrangements. Banks handle this transition differently, but in all cases they aim to eliminate the interest-free nature of the overdraft so you will turn into a profitable customer. Banks are required to notify you, in writing, *well* in advance of the change taking place. Your bank or another bank may offer you a 'graduate loan', which allows you to bring all of your overdrafts together so you only have one. I have been told by numerous people that when they explored this idea, it turned out to be a bad deal, as the interest rate charged on the consolidated overdraft was higher than the individual ones were. A better approach is to pay off the overdrafts, preferably before the new, tougher terms kick in. If you can't pay them all off at once, pay the ones with the highest charges first.

Many students told me about being offered several free overdrafts which they took 'because they were offered'. Once they graduated, they started to get charged interest on them. No one remembered getting warned in advance of the change, but it may be that they just didn't notice (see next sub-section). The interest rates were high, and they had to work hard to pay the balances and interest they had accumulated. They were all pretty cross about their naivety and wondered how they could not have realized these overdrafts wouldn't be free forever. Every one of them said they wouldn't have spent the money they did if they had understood how it worked.

Account controls: reconciliations and errors

The content of this section relates to savings accounts as well as current accounts, but I've included it here because it is more time critical in relation to your current account than to your savings account. There are four things that typically go wrong with a bank account, which you need to be on top of.

The first one is that you can make a mistake. The worst result of a mistake is that you go overdrawn. So this is another reason to keep close tabs on what's going on within your bank accounts. Look particularly carefully at cheques you send to your bank for deposit, as they take a few days to get credited to your account.

The second is that the bank can make a mistake. Money you're sure had gone in doesn't get credited to your account, or payments are taken out of your account that you haven't authorized. Or maybe some money has appeared in your account that you don't recognize – don't spend it if it's not yours! Any of these could be a genuine mistake made by the bank. The key is to find them as soon as possible and take action.

The third is that someone can hack into your account and withdraw money. If this happens, you must react immediately and get in touch with your bank. If you don't, you may be at risk of not having the money that has been taken paid back to you by your bank.

And the fourth is when you see a direct debit that you don't remember authorizing, or standing orders that you thought you cancelled still show up as coming out of your account. You need to catch these early, so that you only have one month's charges to untangle, rather than several months.

Whenever you call a bank, it's likely you'll be calling a large call centre. Bear in mind that the person on the line spends their *entire day* dealing with problems... so try to make it easy for them. Explain your situation fully. Be as precise as possible on dates and amounts, aiming for both of you to have a full understanding of the bank's and your side of the story. Hopefully, the issue will be resolved to your satisfaction. Don't hesitate to ask for compensation if you have incurred a financial loss, and don't be surprised if the bank takes back any financial gain.

If you don't feel the situation has been satisfactorily resolved, you should make it clear to the person that you want to 'file a complaint'. By using that specific wording, you will be letting the bank know that it is a serious problem, and the person on the phone will escalate the issue to their manager. There has been a huge amount of focus on the way banks handle complaints (or don't!) and several have incurred regulatory fines. Banks are required to address any issue raised with them within 80 days. That doesn't necessarily mean giving you what you want, though; it means treating you fairly. If you're not satisfied with how you're treated, you are free to file a further complaint with the Financial Ombudsman Service (FOS). Plenty of people do, so don't be shy about it. The FOS publishes a list of number of complaints by bank twice a year, and the numbers are high. The big three UK-headquartered banks (Royal Bank of Scotland, Lloyds Banking Group, Barclays) tend to head the list every time, but to be fair they do have an awful lot of accounts, so their numbers are bound to be big.

Savings/deposit accounts

Your bank has probably offered you a savings account, and you may want to hold your savings there. But you can put your money into any bank – look for the one with the best interest rate/shortest lock-in periods as described in Chapter 6.

Banks will pay you interest on the money you have in your account. The amount you earn, annualized, is called the AER. The commitments made to you about amounts and timing of interest payments will be documented in writing. In general, interest earned will be calculated and paid monthly, based on the average balance in your account (though some banks use the lowest balance in your account during the month) multiplied by the rate of interest, divided by 12. Right now, the interest rates paid by banks are low for a few reasons. These are: the Bank of England base rate (on which all other interest rates are based) is low; you're taking almost no risk by leaving the money with the bank; and you can access your money whenever you want. In summary, it's convenient and safe to keep any savings you have in a deposit account with your bank, but the interest you earn on those savings will be low as a result.

It's easy to get caught up in trying to find the best deal on a deposit account and lose sight of the *actual difference* it would make in terms of interest you will earn. Let's say you have £1,000 on deposit. If you have that money in a bank for a full year at 2 per cent or 4 per cent interest, you will earn £20 or £40, respectively. That income may be subject to tax, so the difference to you may be even less. If you have £10,000 on deposit for a year, you will earn £200 and £400, respectively. *That* is worth thinking about. But why would a bank offer a rate of interest double that of other banks? Suspicious? The answer is likely to be that a high interest rate is the only way they can attract money in. And that should raise alarm bells with you, as it must mean the bank is higher risk than others. The old risk/reward trade-off again!

Security and technology

You'll probably do most of your banking, other than getting cash, via the internet. That will include giving payment instructions, checking your balance and reviewing transactions. There are masses of criminals perpetually trying to access bank account information. Losses and fraud are becoming commonplace and it's in your interest to be vigilant. You'd be surprised to learn (as I was when I heard this recently) that most hackers get into accounts by guessing people's account passwords, and they do that quite easily. Apparently, people are not too clever in picking their passwords. You know why? Because it's a pain to remember complicated passwords, especially if you have lots of them. Record your passwords somewhere, ensuring they are not easily accessible, and are nowhere near other bank information. I recently heard about an application for storing all your passwords and keeping them safe, available at www.dashlane.com – there are others as well, so explore the options.

Be smart and secure

Protect yourself from becoming a victim of a hacker by:

- Making sure your password has a combination of upper-case letters, lower-case letters, numbers and symbols.

- Never giving information out about yourself or your bank account details to anyone, even if the request is via an e-mail or phone call that is supposedly from your bank.

- Calling or e-mailing your bank independently. If you're contacted by your bank, don't respond to that call or e-mail. Hang up the phone, or ignore the e-mail, and call/e-mail the bank yourself (don't press the dial-back button). When you originate contact, *you* are in control of who you're talking to, but if you're responding to a call or e-mail you can't be sure.

- Accessing your bank's website directly, not through links in e-mails they appear to have sent you.

While we're talking security, let's turn our attention to cash machines:

- Have a good PIN that no one can guess, eg not your birthday.

- Don't give your PIN to anyone, *ever*.

- Change your PIN if, for any reason, you think someone may have it or has figured out what it might be. This is easily done via the internet and at some cash machines.

- Be careful when you're getting money out. If anyone is around you, don't feel awkward about covering your hand as you put your number in. You may feel like a weirdo, but so be it. The same goes for using a PIN with your credit or debit card.

Credit cards

A credit card is issued by a bank or other financial institution (eg VISA, MasterCard, American Express). Unlike a debit card, when you use this card money is not automatically taken out of your account. Instead, every time you use it, the money gets added to a running tally. On a monthly basis, the credit card company will send you a list of transactions and will require you to make a minimum payment – currently around 2.0 per cent of the out-standing balance or £5, whichever amount is greater. You're always allowed to pay more than that minimum amount.

The amount of credit card debt in the UK has reached a very worrying level. Many young people I have spoken with told me that getting multiple credit cards and creating overdrafts were what got them into big financial trouble. They got to the point where they were only able to pay off the monthly interest and none of the balance they owed, so their debt got bigger and bigger!

The financial institution is issuing you with a card because they're willing to lend you money, and they hope to make money from you by charging you interest on the balance outstanding at the end of each month. If you pay the full balance owed every month, you will not incur any interest costs and the bank will make no money from you, only from the seller you purchased from. But if you don't pay the card balance off, you will be charged interest on the balance. The rate of interest charged is currently around 18 per cent per annum for purchases; the issuer is required to contact you if the interest rate changes. You can also find the rate on your monthly statement and on the issuer's website.

As this can be an expensive way of borrowing money, you want to avoid spending so much on the card that you can't pay it off at the end of the month (at least most of the time). The interest is calculated and added to your balance on which the next month's interest is calculated, so you end up paying interest on interest.

If you withdraw cash, however, the rate is likely to be around 27 per cent per annum. Importantly, if you used the card to withdraw cash you will be charged that higher rate on the *full balance* of the card, even if you pay the card balance off fully when the account falls due. Read the card's terms and conditions carefully on this – I know many people who learned this the hard way.

Also, be careful of extra charges for using your card outside of the UK – each time you do, the purchase will attract a foreign exchange fee of between 2–3 per cent of the purchase price. If you take cash from a for-eign ATM, your bank is likely to charge you an additional fee (usually 1.5 per cent), and often the local ATM will levy a further fee. So, taking cash out can be quite expensive and may cost you up to 5 per cent of what you withdraw!

Prior to issuing a card, the issuer will carry out a credit check on you. The issuer will set a credit limit which is the amount you are allowed to have outstanding on it at any time – in effect, the size of the loan the issuer is will-ing to give you. Over time, as you demonstrate you can pay what you bor-row, you will be able to increase that limit.

Did you know?

If you have a £1,000 credit card balance and make the minimum payment required every month, it will take 14 years and 11 months to pay it off. You will have paid £882 in interest.

Each month you will get a statement from the credit card company. It con-tains key information and will look something like Figure 9.1.

The statement will give you a date by which you have to make a payment on the account. As mentioned earlier, you must pay the minimum amount indicated on the statement, but you're allowed to pay as much as you like above that. You can make your payment by sending a cheque, in plenty of time for the company to receive and process it before the payment due date; sending a payment instruction via the internet; having a standing order in place for a monthly fixed payment; or having a direct debit in place to pay the full balance monthly. Don't miss the payment date, as these companies are ruthless about charging you. If you decide to set up a direct debit or standing order, make sure you have enough money in your account to cover the amount on each payment date (shown on the card statement).

You'll receive that statement in advance of the payment due date, which gives you a chance to review the statement in detail, ensuring all of the charges are correct and following up on any incorrect ones before the pay-ment goes out of your account. Make a point of reviewing the credit card statement in detail as soon as you receive it. If the balance looks too big, the first thing to check is that your previous month's payment was pro-cessed in time. (I once forgot to sign the cheque I sent to my credit card company, which I only discovered because the payment wasn't credited on my statement.)

Be aware that some companies you buy goods or services from will charge you a fee for paying with a credit card Annoyingly, you usually don't see this until you are nearly at the end of the buying process. Assuming you want to proceed with the purchase, take a moment to think about the incre-

Figure 9.1   Credit card statement

A. N. Onymous
Flat B
150 Address Road
London
SE28 8BY

(1 of 2)

Cardholder	A N Onymous
MasterCard Number	1111 2222 3333 4444
Total Credit Limit	£7,500

Summary   **26 January 2019**

Balance brought forward from previous statement	£572.89
Payments to your account	£570.58 –
Spending on your account plus any adjustments	+ £841.32

(New Balance   = £843.63)

(Minimum Payment   £18.99)

The Minimum Payment each month will be the greater of:
(i) £5 or the full balance if less.
(ii) 2.25% of that month's balance, including any Instalment Plan balance(s) you have on your account, plus that month's Instalment Plan fee(s).

Your nominated bank account will be debited with the full balance on 10 Feb 2019 or soon after.

If you make the minimum payment of £18.99 and it reaches us on the due date of 20 February 2019 your estimated interest payment next month is £17.73. Please refer overleaf for further details.

02071234560

NameFirstname

bank giro credit

Paid in by _____

Date _____

A N ONYMOUS
1111 2222 3333 4444

Local Bank
Local Town
AB11 2CD

Total Cash

Cheques etc

| Fe | Items |
Please do not write or mark below this line

62-19-70
Sorting code number

99
Transaction code

£ _____

<4422117700009999< 621970+< 99   X

(continued)

Figure 9.1   (*Continued*)

2 of 2

Cardholder	A N ONYMOUS
MasterCard Number	1111 2222 3333 4444

27 December 2018 - 26 January 2019

Trans Date	Post Date		Description	Amount
			BALANCE FROM PREVIOUS STATEMENT	£572.89
26 DEC	27 DEC	00000000	LONDON SOUTH EAST ROAD GBR	9.98
28 DEC	31 DEC	11111111	TRAINLINE REFUND Arbroath GBR	2.31 -
03 JAN	04 JAN	22222222	INTERNET CAFE LONDON SE1	39.00
03 JAN	04 JAN	33333333	STUDENT UNION BAR LONDON SE1	16.00
03 JAN	04 JAN	44444444	ASOS.COM asos.com GBR	23.97
04 JAN	07 JAN	55555555	LV INSURANCE W 01200 234567	237.20
07 JAN	08 JAN	66666666	GREENSMITHS FOOD COMPA LONDON	13.76
10 JAN	10 JAN		DIRECT DEBIT PAYMENT - THANK YOU	570.58 -
09 JAN	10 JAN	77777777	CYCLES R US PETWORTH GBR	97.00
19 JAN	21 JAN	88888888	THE GAS CO thegasco.co.uk. GBR	353.34
20 JAN	21 JAN	99999999	GOOGLE *Google Storage g.co/helppay#GBR	1.59
21 JAN	22 JAN	10000000	MILLAND STORES LIPHOOK GBR	11.25
23 JAN	24 JAN	11000000	THE POST OFFICE LONDON GBR	14.54
23 JAN	24 JAN	11100000	BISTRO 1 LONDON GBR	26.00
			NEW BALANCE	£843.63

If you do not pay off the full amount outstanding, we will allocate your payment to the outstanding balance in a specific order, which is set out overleaf within the summary box section on allocation of payments. The way in which payments are allocated can make a significant difference to the amount of interest you will pay until the balance is cleared completely.

SUMMARY OF BALANCES

BALANCE	MONTHLY INTEREST RATE	ANNUAL INTEREST RATE	INTEREST INCLUDED ABOVE	OUTSTANDING BALANCE
Purchases	1.453%	17.436%	£0.00	£843.63
Advances	1.937%	23.244%	£0.00	£0.00

mental cost before deciding which card to use – a debit or a credit card. And note that some credit cards are more costly than others.

Using a credit card can be a useful money management tool if you pay the balance off before you incur any interest charges. The first reason is due to the time value of money. You get to use the card to buy things all month and only have to pay for those things at the end of the month. Unlike when you use your debit card, you have the use of your money all month rather than paying out cash as you go along. The second reason is that your monthly statement gives you an excellent record of the money you spent, when you spent it and what you spent it on. Note that when you use your debit card you will also see all of your transactions on your bank statement.

Three more things to mention about credit cards:

- **Lost or stolen cards** – as soon as you notice your card(s) are missing or stolen, you should contact the card provider. Once you do, the provider will put a stop on your card, which means it cannot be used. If it has been used by whoever took it, the card company will reverse those charges, as they are fraudulent and the provider is required to bear those costs. The sooner you report the missing card the better – it reduces the cost to the provider and the hassle to you of arranging the reversal of charges. Contacting the provider can be, at least momentarily, challenging, because without the card you won't have the phone number to call readily available (it's on the back of the card) and you probably don't know the card number (I've been caught out on that a few times). If this happens, you can find the helpline number on the provider's website and usually on your statement. It is a good idea to have a list of card helplines somewhere easy to find. But perhaps the best thing is to limit the cards you have, so you will notice if one goes missing.

- **Card protection services** – you can buy a service where you give a company details of your cards, then if your wallet gets stolen, they will handle the cancellation and reissuance of everything. Your bank may provide this service, and there are third-party providers too. Approach these with great doubt and care. It is probably better to keep track of cards and who to call yourself!

- **Payment protection insurance** – this is insurance that card and loan providers offer you so that if, due to ill health, loss of job or some other catastrophic event, you cannot make payments on a credit card, home mortgage or other loan, the insurance company will pay on your behalf. While you will read a great deal about the mis-selling of this product and related claims costing banks billions, it is worth considering if this is protection you *want*. If it is, then use price comparison websites to find the best deal and read the fine print very carefully.

While the credit card company is making money from you if you don't pay your credit card balance on time, they make most of their money from the companies that accept their cards. Every time you use a credit card the provider takes a fee from the company you bought your goods or services from.

Store cards

It's hard to imagine, but in the 1980s the only retail chains in the UK that had store cards were M&S and John Lewis, and in those two stores the only cards you could use were their own. How often, when you go into a high-street shop, do they try to get you to register for one of their cards? Usually they will offer you 20 per cent or more off today's purchases. I don't know about you, but I find that discount makes it really hard to say 'no'. If you say 'yes', though, you'll need to go through their credit check process, which may result in you being turned down. (Read about credit ratings in Chapter 11.)

Why do shops offer these cards? No surprise – it's another way for them to make money – in a kind of bankish way. Usually, there's a finance company behind the company you're buying your goods from. They're hoping that you'll use the store card to make purchases and then be unable to pay off the monthly bill so that they can earn money, in the form of interest, just like any other credit card.

Why would you not want to take up the store card offer? The answer is simple – because of the rate of interest you will be charged. The APR for these cards is currently around 36 per cent, so *significantly* higher than a credit card. So why do people do it? They simply can't bear to miss out on the upfront purchase discount; or they can't borrow the money they need to buy whatever it is they feel they need from anywhere else. The first reason is easy to tackle – do it, pay the bill as soon as it arrives and then put the card somewhere you won't use it ever again. The second reason is *not* a good one – adding to an existing financial problem. The store may well save you from yourself on this one. If they check your credit and see that you are high risk with significant debts already outstanding, they may well turn you down.

Did you know?

Forty per cent of store card users do not know the interest they are being charged.

thisismoney.co.uk

One more reason to avoid these cards – the more cards you have, the harder it is to keep track of where you are financially.

Buying on credit

As you start to buy things like furniture, and other big purchases, you will notice stores offering deals like interest-free credit, pay nothing until two years from now, and so on. Approach these offers with caution.

Why do stores do this? First, they are keen to sell whatever it is they are selling, so they're trying to entice you to buy it by making it easy for you to do so. Maybe they have too much stock and they want to get rid of it, even if they lose money. Or, they could be about to get next year's models in, so they want to shift the old stuff. Second, the seller, or the financing company behind the seller, is hoping to earn interest from you. You need to carefully consider the deal – what are the APR and payment terms? Will you be able to pay the amount back when you want to, or do they lock you in for a period with no early payment allowed? Consider if there is a cheaper way to finance whatever it is you are buying – or save your money until you can pay cash.

Borrowing money from a bank – loans

The subject of bank loans appears in several places in this book because banks are where most of us turn when we need to borrow money. When I say 'bank' I also mean other lenders of money that you'll find if you do an internet search on 'bank loan', 'car loan' or 'personal loan'. In this chapter, we'll focus on what I call planned loans; by that, I'm excluding the short-term financial-crunch need to borrow money described in Chapter 7.

The way banks decide whether they will lend you money, how much they will lend you and the lending terminology used is the same regardless of what you want to borrow the money for. The money principles underlying loans are the time value of money and the risk/reward trade-off. You can easily find the current rates on offer on all types of loans on the internet, searching by type of loan and price comparison sites. It pays to shop around – you don't have to borrow from the bank where you have a current or savings account.

Let's start with a quick recap: banks use the money on deposit that people have placed with them, and lend it on to other people. The strategy employed by banks to make money from this process is straightforward – pay the depositor a lower rate of interest than you charge the borrower. The interest rate a bank will charge to lend you money will reflect the base rate as a starting point, increased to reflect the bank's perception of how risky you are.

That means the bank will consider how likely you are to pay the interest you owe during the term of the loan, as those interest payments come due, and to pay them the full amount of the loan back ('principal') at the end of the term of the loan. The lender's starting point in thinking about lending to you will be to assess your credit worthiness, asking you to provide information and/or using a credit-rating agency (refer to Chapter 11 to read about credit ratings). Loan providers are required by the UK regulator to ascertain that you can 'afford' the loan, so they need to know a lot about you and how you could weather the storms of unemployment, rising interest rates and other things that could impact your ability to pay. You should go through a similar thought process for yourself as you consider taking on debt.

Another factor that impacts a provider's willingness to provide a loan is whether the loan is 'secured', meaning whether the loan is backed by something tangible the institution can get its hands on if you don't pay when you are supposed to. In that circumstance, they would sell on the asset to get the money you owe them. Let's take a mortgage, for example. A mortgage is 'secured' against a property. Therefore, if you fail to meet your interest payments, the bank can force you to sell the property and the proceeds of that sale can be used to pay off the mortgage. When a lender provides a mortgage and the borrower puts down, say, a 25 per cent deposit, the property would have to decrease in value by more than 25 per cent before a forced sale of the property would fail to pay off the entire loan. You can see why the 100 per cent mortgages that used to exist provided lenders with very little security, and negative security if house prices are falling.

Did you know?

A third of young people fear still being in debt at 40. One in five is in debt all the time, a quarter have to borrow cash from parents.

Metro

Personal loans differ from mortgages and other secured loans, because in many cases, the assets the loan is associated with are not containable; that is, you could not sell them on their own (think kitchen upgrade); or the bank chooses not to make the loan specifically secured. Because of the lack of security, personal loans attract higher interest rates than secured loans.

Each type of loan is explored further below.

Personal loans

These loans can be used for a wide range of purposes and you have to explain the purpose in detail to the lender. They are typically for a specific need. A few examples are: buying furniture, paying for a wedding or building a garage. Personal loans are not provided to cover general living expenses.

Car/vehicle loans

Lending institutions will treat these as personal loans, but, as this is the most likely loan you will take out in the near term, I wanted to include additional information about the processes involved. Once you've made a decision to buy a car or another vehicle (read Chapter 10 when you're working through your decision), there are a few ways a bank may get involved; or, you may bypass banks altogether.

If you buy the vehicle directly from another person:

- The seller will want you to pay with a personal cheque, provide a banker's draft (the bank will issue a cheque drawn on your account) or transfer money via your bank, PayPal or another mechanism.

- In order to do that, you will need to have the money in your account already, or you need to get it there. You may need a loan and the money has to be in your account, ready to be paid. Getting a car loan is the same as any other loan. The lender will gather information from other sources to assess your credit worthiness, reaching a yes/no decision.

- The bank will also ask about the vehicle because, while the loan won't be formally secured against the vehicle, the lender will want to get some comfort that, if you don't pay back what you owe, it can force you to sell the car to get back the money it lent you. The bank will also want to see the vehicle's registration papers to confirm that you will have good title to it. Good title means that the person you are buying it from has the right to sell it to you because they legally own it. You will also have to show an MOT (Ministry of Transport) certificate if the car is more than three years old, to demonstrate the car is roadworthy. And you will have to show that you have made arrangements to insure the vehicle. (Insurance is described more fully later.) Insurance is important to the bank because it is loaning you money on an asset and if something happens to the asset, the bank wants to make sure it will still get its principal back. If, for example, the car is written off as a result of an accident, the insurance money will go to the bank to pay off the loan.

- Regardless of where you're getting the money from, the seller will not let you have the vehicle until the money is confirmed as being in their account. So if you do a wire transfer, or provide a cheque, they won't let you have the vehicle until the money is cleared by their bank. Clearing a cheque will take a few days, but a wire transfer will be effective nearly immediately. If you provide a banker's draft, you should be able to take the vehicle when you present the draft.

If you buy the vehicle from a dealer:

- A dealer will typically help you navigate the purchase process, as they are likely to be keen to get the deal completed. While the dealer may offer you funding, the underlying money provider will be a financial services institution.

- You may be offered money via a loan, just like one provided by a bank, or a leasing arrangement. The latter is more common for new rather than used vehicles. Make sure you ask both the dealer and your bank about the cost of the loan they are offering, so that you have a full picture on which to make your decision.

- Buying from a dealership makes finalizing the transaction easier when compared with buying from a private individual, for three reasons: the dealer will have the car's registration documentation; will be able to arrange insurance quickly, although this insurance is typically more expensive than if you arranged it yourself; and perhaps most importantly, the dealer may offer you a guarantee on the vehicle you purchase. That guarantee may provide for engine and other repairs, at no cost to you, during a specified period of time, which helps you with your financial planning.

Did you know?

Today, fewer and fewer young people learn to drive. Just 31 per cent of 17- to 20-year-olds, and 66 per cent of 21- to 29-year-olds held licenses in 2016; in 1994 the respective figures were 48 per cent and 75 per cent.

The Week

Housing loans – mortgages

This is a *huge* topic and is covered in detail in Chapter 10. The same concepts apply here as to the other loans we have covered. You're buying something valuable, and the bank will be interested in: what you will be paying for the property; what the bank's surveyor assesses the property to be worth; and how much money you want to borrow. As with all loans, the bank will want to evaluate your creditworthiness, and that will include assessing your ability to 'afford' the loan – paying the loan and the monthly interest back. Because a mortgage is a long-term proposition (the most common term is 25 years) and lots of things can change over that time period, it is a risky decision for both parties. Therefore, both you and the bank will invest a great deal of time to finalize a deal.

Until recently, banks capped the mortgage loan offered at 75 per cent of the property purchase price or a 25 per cent deposit – the same thing. Now, banks have relaxed their requirements and are more willing to lend with only a 10 per cent deposit. Some banks are now offering 100 per cent mortgages if you have a parent or other relative who is willing to guarantee the mortgage will be paid. As you decide on the loan you want, consider how large a loan you could afford if interest rates increased dramatically. It may be hard for you to imagine, but I can tell you they can change quickly. In the late 1990s, our interest rate went from 8 to 13 per cent in less than a year – nightmare!

Insurance – buying protection

Insurance provides financial protection against a potential future loss. This idea of a potential loss is an important consideration in managing your money effectively. Chances are, the first insurance you will come across is car insurance, which provides protection that your car will be fixed or replaced if you have an accident. You may find that your employer provides you with medical and dental insurance.

Insurance fundamentals

Insurance has a terminology of its own, so let's work through it.

Insurance is a policy you buy on something that's of value to you. You use it to make sure you don't lose out if that something is lost, stolen or damaged. The amount of insurance you take out on the thing of value depends on what the thing is worth; what it would cost to replace. You can insure just about anything. Musicians insure their hands, dancers their legs, horse owners their horses. If you have pets you may have pet insurance, so that if your pet gets ill the insurance company will pay the vet bills.

Life assurance has many of the characteristics of insurance, with the exception that you're not buying protection against a possible future event (death is still inevitable) but merely the timing of it. To keep things simple, I'll explain life assurance as if it were insurance. (On a related note, accidental death insurance provides money if death results from an accident – it is insurance, as it's only a possible event.)

Policy periods and **renewal** refer to the period the insurance coverage will be in place, and therefore, how long you will be expected to pay the premiums (see below). Most policies cover one year, with the option to renew the policy. Often the cost of that insurance will increase when you renew. Put a note in your diary about two months before the renewal is due, and shop around, using internet sites in the first instance. Loyalty does not pay when it comes to insurers!

Premium refers to the payments you make to the insurance company for providing you with the insurance policy. Usually it will be a monthly payment made by cheque or via a direct debit to your bank account. However, you can also make an upfront annual payment. That amount will be less than 12 times the monthly payment amount you are quoted, because you're paying the full amount up front. (This goes back to the time value of money principle.)

Several factors will influence the premium amount, which are the same for all types of insurance, but we will use car insurance as an example (with one small deviation at the end):

- The value of what you're insuring. It's obvious that it is going to cost you more to insure a brand-new Maserati than a 10-year-old Ford Fiesta, or even a new Ford Fiesta. The value of the car is taken into account, as is the cost of repairing the car.

- How good/all-inclusive the insurance policy is. There are two types of car insurance policies – fully comprehensive and third-party. UK law only requires you to have third-party insurance. Fully comprehensive means that the insurance company will cover your costs, as well as the costs of whoever you crash into, if the accident is your fault. Under third-party insurance, the company will only cover the cost of damages to the car/person you crash into. Disappointingly, the cost difference between the two types is negligible these days, because, as I was told by my insurance company: 'We can't estimate the value of what you will crash into.'

- The **excess** level is the amount you will spend on repairs before the insurance company starts to pay up. If you offer to pay the first £200 of expenses to repair your car, your premium will be less than if you have no excess, which means the insurance company pays for everything. If you offer to pay the first £500 of expenses, the premium will be lower than if you have a £200 excess. Many insurance companies are now requiring all young drivers to have a mandatory excess of £300. If you have an accident that costs £199 or £499 to fix, under the two scenarios here, or something just a bit higher than the excess, it may be financially advantageous to pay the repair costs yourself. That may help you avoid having your insurance premium increase in the following year. But chances are, under your policy, you will be required to notify the insurance company of any accident, whether you claim costs back or not, which means you may suffer a premium increase regardless.

- Putting limits on what is covered under the policy will reduce your premium. For example, third-party versus comprehensive coverage for cars. But this is much more relevant to medical insurance. You can get lower premiums if certain medical problems are excluded, because the insurance company will not pay for treatment of those. This is most common where insurance companies may exclude paying you for treatment of any medical conditions that you know of when you sign up for the policy (pre-existing conditions).

The business of insurance providers

Where do you go to get insurance? Some of the main brands you will come across are Aviva, Direct Line, Admiral, Churchill, AXA/PPP and BUPA. Some of these are owned by insurance companies, and some are owned by banks. Supermarkets are increasingly offering these products through arrangements with insurance companies, so next time you go into Tesco or Sainsbury's, take a look at the booklets at the tills. The internet is a great resource for finding the best insurance deals – price comparison sites like gocompare.com, confused.com and comparethemarket.com are easy to find. Lastly, you can go to an insurance broker, which is like a travel agent for the insurance industry.

Insurance providers are in the business of making money. They set premium rates with the expectation that they will receive more money from premiums than they will have to pay out to people claiming on the policies. To increase their probability of getting that right, they assess the likelihood of a bad event happening and factor it into their pricing. They do that based on masses of data. For cars, they have found that younger drivers have more accidents than older drivers. Powerful cars with big engines tend to have more costly accidents than 1.2-litre engine cars that go slower. Cars kept on the street are more likely to get stolen than those parked in garages.

Insurance companies will take this generic information into account, as well as your specific information, when they provide you with an **insurance quote** (pricing proposal). If you've had any accidents, it'll cost you more to insure a car than if you have had none. The same goes for speeding tickets. Getting through the first three years of driving without a traffic violation or accident is a good goal for lots of reasons, including money!

You may think: 'Maybe I'll go without car insurance.' Sorry, you can't; it's against the law for the owner of a car not to insure it. The police use automatic number plate recognition equipment to find uninsured cars as they move around or are parked.

You'll also have to have insurance if you rent a car – if you rent a car you may find that your own car insurance includes rental cover. If you don't, the car rental company will provide it at a cost to you. That's usually an incremental cost to the cost per day you were quoted for the rental, so watch out! If you rent cars often, it's worth considering getting insurance to cover the excess amount that the car hire firm is offering you. Do an internet search on **car excess insurance**. If you plan to drive a friend's car, or let your friend drive your car, talk to the relevant insurance company in advance to make sure the car will be insured – don't assume it is.

Types of insurance

Life

You may not have given much thought to this yet, but you will once other people start to depend on you. Your employer may provide life assurance for you (which will have tax consequences, as noted in Chapter 8). Life assurance provides a lump sum to whomever you have designated to receive it when you die. The sum paid is either described as an amount, or if the assurance is being provided by your employer, it is likely to be stated as a multiple of your base salary. It is very important that the assurance company or your employer has something in writing that states who should receive the money upon your death (your 'beneficiary').

Accidental death

This is a lump-sum payment made to whomever you designate if your death is due to an accident rather than natural causes or illness.

Private medical

As you know, the NHS provides medical services to all of us free of charge (although not totally free as we pay National Insurance and other taxes to fund the NHS). When you travel within the EU, it is a good idea to take your EU medical card (EHIC) with you, as long as we remain EU members. If you get ill or injured when you are on holiday, that will be covered under your travel insurance (see below). But what about when you are here in the UK? What if you don't want to wait for the NHS all the time? What do those doctors do when they are doing private work with private patients?

Private health insurance, or medical insurance, is becoming more common in the UK, as the NHS faces increasing challenges with balancing its costs and the services it provides. An increasing number of companies are providing it to their employees, and an increasing number of people are buying it for themselves. If you have 'private' medical insurance, you will still need to see a GP in the first instance – either your NHS one or a private one (at your expense) who will then refer you to a specialist. It is seeing the specialist and having additional tests and other procedures performed under his or her direction that this insurance covers. Do make sure you get any treatment pre-approved by the insurance company, which should only take a phone call to arrange. This insurance also covers surgery in private hospitals and will usually result in your being treated more quickly than under the NHS, particularly for those medical treatments that are not 'life critical'.

Private dental

This type of insurance is being sought by more people as it gets increasingly difficult to get NHS dental care. As with health insurance, people are turning to private dentists and looking to insure themselves against those potential costs. A common provider is Denplan, though a selection can be found using insurance websites like moneysupermarket.com.

Travel

If you have done much travelling on your own you're probably aware of this insurance. It provides protection if your trip is cancelled, if you cannot go through with your plans for medical reasons, if you lose something while travelling or if you get ill while in a foreign country. (It's best to always charge a trip or flight to a credit card, if possible, as you then have additional protection, eg if the travel firm goes bankrupt you are more likely to get your money back than if you paid cash or with a debit card.) You need to read the small print carefully to make sure you understand what is and what is not covered. High-risk sports like hang-gliding are frequently excluded; skiing and scuba-diving frequently require additional premium payments.

Travel insurance can be purchased for one trip only, for multiple trips or for a period, typically a year. Most travel insurance policies won't cover you if you are going to be travelling for more than 90 consecutive days.

Home and contents

Home insurance is designed to protect you if your home is damaged or destroyed, and contents insurance covers you for damage, destruction or theft of everything that is inside the home.

Once you own a home, as opposed to renting it, you will have to arrange home insurance. This will be required by the mortgage lender if you have taken out a loan. This is because the lender has secured the loan against that property and therefore will want to make sure that its value is maintained. The lender always wants to make sure the property is in a state where, at a push, it could be sold to pay off the mortgage. So, if your home was totally destroyed, the insurance company would pay you the committed amount so that the money would be used to rebuild the home or pay off the mortgage.

Contents insurance protects you from losses incurred if your possessions are damaged, destroyed or stolen. Take a moment to think of all the stuff you have and how much it would cost to replace it. Under this type of insurance policy, you insure for an overall amount and you can also insure specific items. A family heirloom, an expensive piece of jewellery, artwork or other valuable items need to be mentioned to the insurer, so that they price that into the contract. Check to make sure that your possessions are covered by the policy even if they are outside your home.

It is likely that your family's contents insurance will cover your possessions when you are away at college or university. However, you need to check it out. It's also likely that the insurance policy requires you to lock your room, flat or house, or bike or car, to protect them from thieves. If you don't do that, the insurance firm is unlikely to pay up. In the event something gets stolen or damaged, report it to the insurance company immediately. They may ask you to provide a police report, which means you need to call the police immediately too. (As an aside, if you are burgled and it looks like the burglar is still on the premises, do not enter the premises for safety reasons.)

Professional indemnity

If you are a budding entrepreneur running your own business, you will be providing services and/or products to clients. That means you will need insurance to protect you against any claims those clients make against you. They typically include negligence, non-delivery on commitments, and mistakes. I wanted to make you aware of this, hence the mention, but that is all I will say about it.

There you are. The financial fundamentals you need to know. There are others, of course, throughout this book, so keep reading!

10
Making big
financial decisions

Chances are that most of your money decisions so far have been fairly straightforward and short-term. Most of the effort you spend on managing your money may be aimed at working out how to get from month to month; keeping your inflows and outflows of cash in sync during the month; and perhaps trying to figure out how to earn more money without sacrificing other parts of your life.

In this chapter, we will look at some of the bigger and longer-term money decisions you're likely to make. As a large proportion of your earnings is likely to be spent on housing costs, this chapter covers the issues of renting, buying and comparing finances across the two.

To clarify, 'bigger' here means making a decision that involves saving money, borrowing money or spending a substantial amount of money, and 'longer' means making a decision that commits you to making ongoing payments or having money tied up in something for a long time. Some of these decisions will feel complicated, especially as there's lots of new terminology that people will use. Don't let that get to you or let yourself feel pushed into a decision before you are ready. Ask questions, take your decision step by step and you will figure it out.

Where to go for guidance

Think about a time in your life when you thought 'I can't figure this out'; and somehow, you did. Look back on that to give you confidence that you'll be able to figure out anything financial. When you're making money decisions, here are a few places to get help:

- **Family** – this includes aunts, uncles, brothers, sisters, cousins and even parents. Parents like to be asked for advice and generally do recognize that things have changed since they were your age. Family friends are also a good avenue to explore.

- **Friends** – these can be a great resource, especially if they have been through a similar decision and perhaps are a little older.

- **The internet** – how did we survive without the internet?! You can access tons of information to help you – almost too much. I suggest you just jump in and start looking; start with general searches and then narrow your search down. Use searches like 'How do I buy a scooter?' 'What are the steps in the flat rental process?' 'What do I need to know when I look for car insurance?' – you get the idea. Keep notes of sites you used and what you learned, so you can refer back to what you found.

- **Visit providers** of whatever it is you are thinking about spending money on. You want to buy a car? Go to car showrooms and find someone who is willing to take the time to explain everything you need to know about cars and financing options. You want to buy a flat? Do the same at estate agents, lawyers and surveyors. Need to borrow money? Go to your bank and other banks to ask about financing terms. And in any of these places, if the people you talk to say things or use words you don't understand, get them to stop and explain.

You may hesitate to ask questions, thinking 'I should know' or 'they're busy', but let me share a secret with you. People love to talk about what they do. And that's what you're asking them; it gives them a chance to share what they know! Do a bit of research before you start your visits, so you look serious about whatever it is. Invest time in planning for those sessions so you can make the most of them.

Let's now take a look at some of these big and/or long-term decisions, going from smaller to larger money amounts.

Inadvertent commitments

There are several ways you can end up committing to something that, while not a lot of money in the big scheme of things, may be long-term and therefore lock you into a spend. Think free offers, magazine subscriptions, gym membership, or buying one of those restaurant and club cards that gives you discounts. What experiences do you have of committing to something that was a bit longer-term than you realized? Did you have any trouble ending the contracts… or is it just me?!

Most of these commitments will run for a year, but the onus is usually on you to cancel the contract when the year is up. In order to avoid an automatic renewal you don't want, make a note in your diary a month before the year runs out and send an e-mail to cancel the contract. Then, check your bank account to make sure it is cancelled!

Transport – bikes

Bikes are increasingly used as a means of transport, particularly in big cities. The range of what you can spend is huge, and being tough with yourself when you're deciding how much to spend is well worth the time. Include thoughts about how tempting it will be to thieves in your calculations. You'll need insurance if you don't have it, or it's not included in your (or your parents') home contents insurance. You'll need a really good lock, and must use it *all the time*. Insurance companies are unlikely to reimburse you for a stolen bike if it wasn't locked.

If you're going to use your bike for transportation (ie beyond exercise), you may need to own a bike, but if you're in a city you can consider renting bikes when you need them. In London and other UK cities there are Santander bikes that are easy to rent. You download the app onto your phone and register a debit card to be able to use them. The cost is £2 for a day, and any journey of less than 30 minutes is included in the £2. There are an increasing number of 'dockless' bikes available. As with Santander bikes, you download the app, register a debit card and you're all set. The app will show you where the nearest bike is, and you'll be charged based on the duration of your journey. Be sure to leave it in a thoughtful place (not the middle of the pavement), and in an 'approved zone' (as explained on the website).

Transport – cars, motorcycles and scooters

What do you need to think about when you are buying a scooter, motorcycle or car? The first thing, of course, is how much you can spend on buying it – the purchase price. How much money do you have? Do you need a loan? Who should the loan come from?

There are quite a few other costs that you need to take into account, in addition to the purchase price. These will vary for the three types of vehicle but in principle they are similar. They include:

- **Fuel** – a fuel-efficient car will save you money. Your options are petrol, diesel (encouraged by the government until recently), hybrid and electric. Electric cars will run out of charge after an estimated number of miles that will be clearly disclosed – they can be recharged at power points or at your home, both of which cost money. You will want to consider how much driving you plan to do and calculate the cost of fuel, the cost of vehicle tax and the purchase price.

- **Repairs** – engine repairs, replacement tyres, oil changes and other servicing work, to keep it working well, will all have to come out of your cash flow so need thinking about. In general, diesel engines last longer than petrol engines. Electric cars have fewer parts, so may have fewer repairs, but as they're new no one is certain of that.

- **Insurance** – this was covered in detail in Chapter 9. Remember that you'll want to have some money in reserve to cover the excess, or repair costs you want to pay for yourself, in the event of an accident.

- **Vehicle tax** – when you buy a car, you will need to pay tax on it. The amount of tax varies based on the size of the engine and the government's view of its environmental impact. Currently the annual tax due can range between £0 and more than £2,000, so tax may be a critical factor in your decision. Take a look at https://www.gov.uk/vehicle-tax-rate-tables to see the fee for your car, motorcycle or scooter. You need to pay the tax before you drive the car, otherwise you can get fined.

- **MOT** – if your car is more than three years old you will need to have an MOT (see direct.gov.uk for a full explanation), which is an annual test conducted by a garage to certify that your car is roadworthy. Mine always seems to need something done to be roadworthy! You need to factor the cost of the test and any repairs that may be needed into your budget. Don't even *think* of driving without a valid MOT; as with road tax, having a valid MOT is a legal requirement – the fine for not having one is £1,000.

- **Parking** – consider where you will keep the vehicle. Can you park it for free, or will you need to rent a parking space?

If you decide that owning a car is too expensive, particularly for the amount you will use it, there are a variety of rental alternatives. There are daily car rental companies – eg Hertz, Avis, Enterprise, as well as local firms. There are also firms that provide rentals on an hourly basis, though so far only in big cities, and for those you pay only for the time you actually use the car (eg easyCar, Zipcar). There are also peer-to-peer rentals (eg WhipCar, Drivy and Hiyacar). Do be sure to ask about additional charges they may put on if you are a young driver. And look out for insurance costs!

If you decide to buy a car and find you don't use it as much as you planned, you can rent it out to others for hours or days. This would make you a *provider* in the peer-to-peer market, which is mentioned above.

Buy new or used?

A big decision is whether to buy a brand-new or used car. For the most part, and particularly if you have limited funds, it makes little economic sense to buy brand new, as that car will lose value as soon as you take it off the forecourt! Do get an independent mechanic or the Automobile Association or Royal Automobile Club to check out your car before you buy it. A shiny-looking car can have all sorts of mechanical problems that you don't want to be surprised by. You may find a used car dealer is the best option for you, if the dealer offers you a great price, good financing through a leasing agreement and the peace of mind of having a warranty that covers repairs for the first few years.

The important thing is to shop around a lot, see what offers the car dealers can give you, and look at the current price of similar cars that are on the used-car market. Do remember you can go to a car auction, though do take a mechanic with you to check the car out before you buy.

Financing options

There are several ways to finance a car purchase which are explained in Chapter 9. In a nutshell, you can pay cash, get a loan or take a lease from the dealer.

Gap year or gap months

For those people who take gap years (pre- or post-university), the preparation and travel can be a great financial learning opportunity, as well as learning about other things, of course. If you're going to take a gap year trip, you'll need to figure out where you want to go, how much money you'll need, who you'll travel with, and what you want to do during those travels. Armed with your 'money needed' figure, you'll have to figure out how to earn it and how to save for it. It can be a great test of your willingness to forego short-term pleasures for a long-term goal.

Keep in mind that as you earn money, taxes are likely to be withheld, so figure that into your planning. A few people told me that they purposely let the employer collect the tax monies, even though they knew they would get the money back later, as it was a way of forcing them to save. When they left on their travels, they filed their tax reclaim and were happy to have money in their bank when they returned from their trip. If you don't want income tax withheld as you earn, learn what steps to take in Chapter 8.

While gap months/years have typically been taken around university time, it can be done whenever you want. Once you get into the work/career thing, of course, it can be more complicated to plan. If you're thinking of taking time off work, talk to your employer early on about your thoughts. There are a few additional questions you'll want to consider: Is this the right time to do this? What am I planning to get out of the travel? What will happen to the job I'm postponing or stepping away from? What impact will this have on my career? Can I take my full personal leave time for the year all at once, and supplement it with some unpaid leave? There are some careers/companies that offer paid or unpaid sabbaticals as a matter of course, ranging from several months to a year.

Two important things to mention: 1) when buying airline tickets for a long multi-step trip, it is usually less expensive to buy a round-the-world ticket (currently around £1,300) than individual tickets. And 2) check out your travel insurance to make sure your whole trip is covered, as many policies don't cover you if you travel for more than 90 days in one go.

University – go, no go, alternatives?

The cost of going to university in England and Wales has tripled in the past few years (for Scottish residents attending university in Scotland there is no tuition cost). Historically, there was a general view that university graduates would quickly out-earn their contemporaries who did not go to university. With unemployment and underemployment among young adults increasing, there are more questions being asked about the value of higher education.

Let's concentrate on the financial issues. In England and Wales, the first time that university students were required to pay for their tuition was in September 1998, and the maximum they could be charged was £1,000 per year. In 2004 that amount was increased to £3,000, and in 2008 it went up to £3,290. From September 2012, universities were permitted to charge up to £9,000 a year for tuition; this was later increased in 2016 to its current level of £9,250. In addition, students need to cover living expenses, which, depending on where in the UK you are living, typically run between £150 and £250 a week.

The government has established loan programmes to support university students. There are two useful places to look for information: https://www.gov.uk/student-finance and https://www.slc.co.uk/students-and-customers.aspx. Explore these costs early if you are thinking of going to university! The key points to be aware of are:

- Full-time students may take out government loans for the full amount of tuition fees, up to a maximum of £9,250 per year; part-time students may be eligible to borrow up to £6,935 per year. The tuition fee loan is paid from the government directly to the university and you'll be required to pay the loan back.

- Students may be eligible to receive maintenance loans to help them with living costs. The amount you may be provided with changes annually, so check out the website referred to above. Maintenance loans are subject to means testing, ie based upon your family income, and these details are available on the website. The maintenance loan money is paid directly to your bank account at the beginning of each academic term – so you need to manage that money carefully to last you all term. You will be required to pay the loan back.

- It is also possible to obtain additional government funds for tuition and maintenance expenses if your family income is low or for other reasons detailed on the government's student finance website. There's also the possibility that your university might offer you a bursary, so, if finances are an issue, do explore that avenue as well.

Once again, these loans will have to be paid back. At the bottom of the student finance page noted above is a section titled 'More Useful Links', and the second item you'll see and should click on is 'Paying back your student loan'. This will take you to a page that explains the repayment process.

> **TIP**
>
> If you are a university student, take advantage of student discounts in shops and get an NUS Extra card, which offers more than 200 discounts at chains ranging from Superdrug to National Express and costs £12.

Once you finish university, you'll be liable for the total amount you borrow under these loan arrangements. The arrangements differ depending on whether your course began before or after 1 September 2012, so make sure you look at the right webpage. If, when you finish university, you have cash which you could use to pay off your student loan, think carefully. If the rate of interest you pay for the loan is less than the interest rate you can get on savings, you'll be making money by letting the loan continue. And you may want to keep the cash lump sum ready for another use – say making a deposit on a property – so if you use it to pay off your loan it won't be there when you want it. And once you do have excess cash, always pay off the most expensive loan first, which may or may not be this one.

Key points about student loans

- Interest is added to the initial loan amount from when you get the money. The Student Loan website sets out the interest rates and provides information on how repayments are calculated.

- The government will collect the money from you via payroll deductions (explained in Chapter 8) once you are earning more than £18,330 a year (if you started your course before 1 September 2012) or more than £25,000 (if you started after 1 September 2012). The repayments will be deducted from your gross pay (see Chapter 8) from the April after you leave university. You can make additional payments if you wish to repay your loan earlier – which you may want to do if you have access to money that costs less to borrow.

- You should receive an annual statement of your loan situation from the Student Loans Company, but you can check your balance online at any time, as explained on the website.

Several people told me that they wish they had done paid work while they were at university. They figured it definitely would have been doable with a bit of self-discipline. They also mentioned that by working part-time they would have avoided spending money on going out as much – a double bonus!

Owing to the increased university costs, students are considering other educational options such as vocational learning offered at colleges, which includes a wide range of courses, involving practical experience organized by the college. Some professions, such as accountancy, are establishing apprentice programmes as an alternate route into an accounting firm. When thinking about the finances of university, both in earnings and in expenditures, use the web to your advantage and fully research your options.

Did you know?

Sixty-seven per cent of millennials who went to university think they didn't benefit from their studies. Thirty-five per cent wish they hadn't gone while 48 per cent believe they would now be earning more had they not done so.

The Week

University later

Many of the young people I coach feel or felt pressured to go to university right after sixth form. Several of them came out not knowing how to use their degree, or what sort of jobs (notice I did not say careers) to start in. Some of them have told me that, on reflection, they wish they had waited a few years and applied to university having been out in the world of work a bit. So if you feel pressured to go, but are uncertain about whether it's what you really want to do at this time in your life, be brave and stand up for what you want.

All about housing

Chances are your first *big* financial decision has been, or will be, about where to live once you have moved away from home. If you go to/are at university, you'll probably have to figure out your own accommodation. And at some point, you may look to buy a property. Either way, you'll need to think about who you share living space with, so we'll start there.

Deciding who to share with

The first and most important thing to think about for many reasons is who you want to share with, and how many of you will be in one property. In some ways, sharing with more rather than fewer people is good, because you can share costs. On the other hand, sharing with a big group can make household arrangements like paying shared bills, cleaning the place and keeping the kitchen in order a nightmare.

Among the many things you want to think about when picking people to share with is whether your money values are similar. For example: Do they spend money on the same things as you do? Are they big spenders compared with you? Are you on a tight financial package compared to them? Or perhaps it is the other way around: Are you flush with money and they aren't? What will you do if they have to move out? Are they likely to honour their rental commitments for the full period of the lease?

We often make assumptions about these values, or simply don't consider them; and then things can go badly wrong. What have I seen? Someone who let the others down on a one-year lease by not turning up for university – and left her friends to cover her costs. Disagreements over noise levels. Most often, disagreements about how tidy or not the place was kept. I've also heard about people not paying their share of bills on time, so others had to pay more to avoid losing their electricity.

Another thing to consider is room allocations. Will you all pay the same rental amount if not all bedrooms and bathroom arrangements are equal? How will you decide who gets which room? Is it useful to consider what year 2 in the same place could mean for room allocations in year 1? Will you switch rooms and/or change rental amounts in year 2?

You can't really ask the person you're hoping to share a place with what they will be like to live with… but you *can* reduce the risk of a clash. Talk about lifestyles – eg big partyers or not, hard workers or not, tidy or untidy, early risers or late-night people? As you think about these questions, you may figure out that you can't live with some of your friends – but at least they will stay your friends! Several people I spoke with said they thought it was easier to have negotiations over money and other things with acquaintances than it was with friends. Make sure you organize a watertight lease for all the sharers to sign, and have their parents sign... though even that doesn't guarantee that everyone will deliver on their commitments.

Renting property

The all-in cost

Once you've figured out who you want to live with and how much you want to spend, you can start looking for a property. Use the internet, look in local newspapers, look in estate agents' windows and register with them as well, to search for what you want. Also talk to friends who are a little older and have recently been through the same experience. If you don't have people you want to share with, you can identify places to share using websites like flatshare.com, roommates.com, sofasurfer.com, gumtree.com and plenty of others. Be careful, though – do not pay any money over until you *see* the property you're planning to rent, even if the person says there is 'lots of interest and you may not get it if you don't pay now!'.

Comparing rental property prices is not as straightforward as you'd expect. Be careful comparing weekly with monthly prices – it's easiest to turn those into an annual number to start. You need to figure out what the *total* cost will be, asking questions of the agent and existing tenants and exploring for yourself, including:

- How long is the lease? If you're only going to need the property for eight months while you're at university, do you have to take a 12-month lease? Can you sublet some rooms to other people for the last four months?

- How much money do you have to pay to get the property? Landlords often require two months' rent up front, when you sign the lease. One month is for the landlord to keep as a deposit to use if they need to fix things when you move out (see below) and the other is the first month's rent. You always pay rent one month in advance of when you're using the property.

- Is it furnished or unfurnished? Renting unfurnished is straightforward – there will be nothing there when you move in except 'white goods' (fridge, cooker, oven and maybe a washing machine or dishwasher). A furnished place is less straightforward. Be absolutely certain, before you sign the lease, as to what furniture comes with the property – ask for the list in writing. If there's someone living there, don't assume all that you see is included. Even if it *is* furnished, you'll typically still need to add things like kitchen chairs, a table, a desk, bookshelves, an ironing board, a vacuum cleaner (that works) and a reasonably sized kitchen bin. Check out the kitchen equipment, eg plates, cutlery, pans, to make sure there is enough for the number of you living in the place. Check out the curtains or other window coverings. Confirm whether bed and bath linen is included.

- What's the cost of utilities and are they included in the rental price? Usually the tenant is responsible for the cost of electricity, gas, water, and heating of whatever type. Ask what you can expect the monthly bills to be. Ask about the winter and summer costs, as you may be surprised by the difference. Remember to think about internet connections, TV, and a phone landline if you need one.

- Are you liable for council tax/rates? The estate agent should be able to tell you these amounts, and in some places it can be surprisingly high, eg Scotland. The tax is what you pay for local services, such as rubbish collection. While you are a student, you're likely to be exempt, but to get the exemption you'll need to complete paperwork to notify the council of your student status. If you have students and non-students in your place, the council will give you a reduced rate, but again, you have to notify the council to get the reduction. If you have a student and non-student mixed household, you'll need to agree up front who will be paying the tax (ie will you share the cost, or will the students not pay any?).

- Do you need insurance? Think about what you'll do if something happens to the property and the stuff in it. Will your parents' home insurance pay the cost of replacing anything that is destroyed or stolen? If you're a student, the answer to this last question is likely to be yes. The landlord is responsible for insuring the building – though dilapidations are your responsibility (more on that later).

- What else might cost you money that you need to ask about? A lovely garden that you need to contribute running costs to? Someone to clean the entrance? Any sort of maintenance? When you're renting, those costs should be covered by the landlord, but it is best to be certain.

Signing a lease

This too can become more complicated than you expect. It's worth asking one of your friends who has done it before, or your parents, or someone else you trust, to review the document. In a nutshell, the lease commits you to do certain things – eg pay rent, maintain the property in good condition, not put holes in walls to hang pictures, not sublet the property. In return the landlord lets you live there. It seems a bit one-sided and that is how it will read – lots of obligations on your part and few on the landlord's part.

But they *are* responsible for ensuring that the house is safe to live in, and for repairing things that break.

Before you sign the lease, make sure the property has what you need in it, as you'll be signing to take the property on *as it is* unless specified. Once you sign the lease, the landlord is unlikely to do anything to address what you want, eg put in smoke alarms, repair anything that is not working, provide additional furniture and so on. If you're in Scotland, make sure that any property is HMO (Houses in Multiple Occupation) licensed; and similarly in England, if five or more people are going to live together.

For university student rentals, it can be common for landlords to offer nine- or twelve-month leases. To be honest, if they offer a nine-month lease, it is usually the same total cost as for a full year, just divided by fewer months. For other rentals, it's common practice to have a one-year lease with a six-month break clause, which enables either the landlord or the tenant to end the agreement any time after six months. The person ending the arrangement typically has to give two months' notice in writing. That means that a six-month lease becomes an eight-month commitment. Read this part of the lease very carefully.

If you're renting with others, you'll have to decide collectively how you are going to be held together legally to meet the lease commitments. You can have one person sign the lease, which means that person is liable for the property and lease. Everyone else is obligated to him or her to abide by the terms of the lease. If you do it this way, you should put something in writing for each person to sign to demonstrate their commitment to do what is expected. The alternative is that each person signs his or her own lease with the landlord. The landlord is very likely to have a view on this – typically, they'll want the former, so their life is easier.

One more thing to consider in the lease is what the lease renewal clause says. What you're looking for, whether or not you plan to stay for longer than the proposed lease term, is an option to renew the lease. And you want the clause to state that the rental increase for the new lease will be limited – typically to the increase in inflation or the Retail Price Index, both of which you can find on the internet. Without this clause, the landlord will legally be able to set the new rental rate at whatever they want.

Moving in

Right, you have rented your perfect place (or the best you can afford) and it's moving-in day. Congratulations! You'll have organized the electricity, water, and anything else to be changed to your/someone's name. The landlord/

agent should have helped with that, as the previous tenant will have re-moved their name from the bills. Don't get too upset if, when you walk in, the place doesn't look the same as it did before; empty places nearly always look worse than occupied ones.

It's *critical* that you do a detailed moving-in inventory that lists every-thing in the place and the condition of the accommodation, including what you see behind and under furniture. At the risk of being unfair, I have found university-town estate agents to be rubbish at this when you move *in*, but really good at finding everything they think is wrong when you move *out* – and charging you for it. So, before you move all your stuff in, walk around the place looking carefully. The agent should have given you a list of the condition of the property and the contents. As you walk around, make sure that the list includes details – a hole in the wall where a picture was, a bro-ken shelf, a door that doesn't close quite right. If the place is furnished, the list should include everything in there, down to the last spoon and plate, so check those details carefully. Check the loos are flushing, the kitchen equip-ment works, and electric plugs work. Document what you find *in detail*, including taking photos.

Pay particular attention to holes or marks on the walls from pictures and posters. If the lease says you can't make holes in the walls or use sticky stuff to put posters up, don't put anything on the walls without the landlord's permission. If you do, you could end up with a large redecoration bill. I re-cently found a solution for this – 3M Command Strips – check them out!

Moving out

It would be unfair for me to say that everyone renting a place gets ripped off when they move out, but it happens an awful lot. If the property is not in the same condition as it was when you took over the lease (notwithstanding reasonable wear and tear), the landlord is entitled to withhold money from the deposit you paid.

You can take steps to ensure that your exit from a property is free of fi-nancial penalties. The biggest issue that arises is a disagreement about the condition of the property when the lease started, which you'll have avoided if you followed the recommendations in the section above. Your aim is to leave it in great shape – what you would want if you were moving in. The other issue is that people often don't plan their move out in advance, so it is a mad rush, with no time to clean the place, repair any damages, or do other things to avoid penalties. So, the first point is *think ahead*. You and your friends have to plan backwards from when you have to be out of the property, and allow plenty of time to get it into a landlord-ready state. Start with the end-of-lease date and plan a good chunk of time for cleaning.

Since it's easier to clean if the place is empty, figure out how/if you can get your stuff out. If you can't get the stuff out, at least move it so you can clean around it. You really have to clean *everything* – crumbs out of drawers, skirting boards, windows, curtains. It takes a huge amount of time to do this well. Because of this, you may find that the lease requires a cleaning by professionals, and that you have to bear the cost. You can reduce this cost by doing the best job you are capable of before the professionals turn up; and try to arrange it so that they charge you by the hour rather than a fixed rate. If the landlord doesn't require a professional clean, they will check it out after you do your clean and charge you for any additional cleaning that needs to be done. You absolutely want to have someone from your group there when you check out, which is when the landlord or their checker will identify what they think counts as dilapidations or things that need further cleaning. If you're not there to discuss or document differences of opinion, you won't be in a good position to challenge the decisions later.

You also need to read and report your water and electricity meters, and notify the providers that you're moving on. You don't have to worry about the new people, but you do have to worry about getting final bills, and ensuring that you don't keep getting bills after you move out. The bills you received during the rental will have the number to call to make these arrangements, and will include the account number and an account holder's name. That 'account holder' will be the person who set up the accounts, and will have to be the one doing the calling. Owing to the Data Protection Act/ GDPR, the utilities companies will not talk to anyone else.

Buying a property

Despite what we read in the papers about a generation that won't own homes, young people are still finding ways to buy them. They do it by cutting out all of their spending for a few years to save for a deposit; they borrow deposit money from friends; they save money in a Buy to Let ISA; or they get lucky and their parents can lend them some money. Saving for a deposit is just the beginning – there are the ongoing mortgage payments, repairs and so on to deal with. While you may feel pressure to buy a home, do remember that house prices can go down as well as up (some of my friends still dispute this despite the facts), and when you want to sell your home, finding a buyer may not be easy.

You may feel pressured to buy, hearing people say things like 'Renting is throwing money away' and 'The cost of renting is the same as owning/paying a mortgage'. That first statement is merely a value judgement. There are many reasons to rent rather than buy, money being just one of them. The second statement may or may not be factual, although I often hear it said. In this section of the chapter we will review all of the expenses involved in buying a property, as we did for renting in the previous section.

When you're making a 'rent versus buy' decision, you have to consider some things that are totally known and some that are not, for which you'll have to form a view about the future. The two things you'll have to take a longer-term view on are: what do you think will happen to interest rates, and what do you think will happen to property prices? The first will directly impact the cost of owning, as you'll have to service your mortgage. The second will directly impact the potential capital appreciation of your property, ie the price when you eventually sell it compared with the price you paid to buy it. If the ongoing costs of renting and buying are exactly the same, but you think that the price of property is going to increase, you would lean towards buying a property, as you could make money when you sell it. Alternatively, if the ongoing costs are the same and you think property prices are going to go down, you would lean towards continuing to rent rather than buy.

In addition to financial thoughts, there are other life events that you may want to factor into a potential property purchase decision, which include:

- What would happen if, a certain number of years after moving in, you lost your job?
- What would you do if you were offered a job overseas, or in another city?
- What would happen if you got into a relationship where you wanted to live with your partner? And what if that partner owned a property too, or lived in another city?
- What if your employer moved to another part of town or to another town?

Despite the UK cultural bias towards owning, renting is a good option in many respects. The two best aspects are: you can be confident of what your monthly costs will be; and if something breaks, the landlord has to fix it. Renting also gives you a great deal of flexibility. With six- or twelve-month leases being the norm, you won't be tied into the arrangement for too long. In your early years of post-college/university work, renting is particularly attractive from a budgeting and cash-flow perspective.

Compare ongoing owning versus renting costs

In the renting section you learned about the all-in costs of renting a home – eg rent, utilities, council tax. If you're starting to evaluate the rent/buy decision, you need to do a full comparison – list, item by item, the costs to you of each of the two options. Let's start by considering the ongoing costs if you buy/own a home – you know the costs of renting already.

When people say that the cost of owning is the same as renting, they are usually just comparing a rough estimate of monthly mortgage payments, but none of the other costs. And, while this is likely to be the biggest cost, the other things do add up.

The primary ongoing costs once you own a property include the following.

Mortgage payments   This is the amount you pay the bank (monthly) for the loan they have given you to buy the property. The amount paid is determined based on the amount of money you borrow (the principal), the type of mortgage (most likely repayment) and the interest rate on the loan. A bank is required by regulation to ascertain that you'll be able to meet your mortgage payments as they fall due. That means your monthly payments and, if you do have an interest-only mortgage, the principal at the end of the mortgage term.

Key mortgage terms to understand include:

- **Salary multiple** – the starting point for banks, when they're deciding how much money they will lend you, is your base salary. The maximum amount they'll lend you is typically expressed as a multiple of your salary – currently most banks offer 4.5 times your salary. Owing to regulatory changes in 2014, a lender has to do enough analysis of your financial position to be certain that you can 'afford' the loan. They will look at what you earn and will ask detailed questions about what you spend your money on. They will also consider your ability to pay your mortgage if interest rates increase – something you should already have done.

  Lenders prefer to lend to people who have been working for a while (say a year) and who are employed by a company rather than self-employed. This is because it's easier for them to confirm what you say you are paid, and having regular salary payments makes them more confident that you'll be able to make your payments.

- **Deposit** – the bank will also require you to provide a lump sum of cash towards a home purchase. For new buyers, this is currently around 10–15 per cent of the purchase price, although this will vary by lender, with some accepting just a 5 per cent deposit. There are some lenders that will allow your parents' financial position to be considered, or allow them to guarantee the loan. The deposit provides protection for the bank; they want to be sure that if you can't meet your payments, your home can be sold, by them, and they will get all of their money back. If you have paid a 15 per cent deposit, they only have to sell it for 85 per cent of the original price to recover all their money.

The government is trying to help first-time homebuyers, and has set up a few programmes under help-to-buy and shared ownership schemes. If you are considering buying a home and it is your first or you earn a low income, you should check out the government programmes on their website: gov.uk/affordable-home-ownership-schemes.

- **Fixed rate interest versus variable rate interest** – there are many different types of mortgage products, and particularly mortgage rate options, on the market, but at the end of the day they come down to types of interest rates – fixed or variable. With a fixed rate mortgage, you agree at the beginning of the loan what the interest rate will be for a set period of time. This means you'll know exactly what your monthly payments will be. You have to pay for that certainty, so the interest on these will be higher than a variable rate mortgage. The set period of time is rarely more than three years, and more typically two years. Look carefully at what happens at the end of the fixed term.

  With a variable rate mortgage, you agree to having the rate of interest you pay change over the term of the mortgage in relation to a specified benchmark. The benchmark is typically the Bank of England lending rate, or it may be a 'tracker' that aligns with movements in the stock market. Obviously, this means that you can't predict exactly what your mortgage payments will be, so it can cause you some cash management angst. Banks must communicate rate changes either in a letter to you or by publication in a major newspaper as detailed in the terms and conditions of the loan – the change won't happen overnight.

  As mentioned before, when you decide to buy a place, you'll need to take a view on what interest rates will do. If you choose a variable rate mortgage, you have a risk that the rate will go up, but you could benefit from the rate going down, as many homeowners did when interest rates plummeted during the financial crisis. Interest rates can change dramatically – in the late 1980s, mortgage rates were 15 per cent!

- **Principal (or capital) repayment mortgage versus interest only** – it is highly likely that you'll only be offered a capital repayment mortgage, which means that each monthly payment you make will be composed of two components – interest on the loan and a repayment of the underlying loan. If you keep the mortgage until the end of its term (usually around 25 years), you will have repaid the full loan amount through these payments. With an interest-only loan, your monthly payments are composed only of the interest, none of the principal.

- **Offset mortgage** – if you keep your savings and hold a mortgage with the same bank, you may be offered this type of mortgage. In this instance, the bank calculates interest daily, and when the calculation is done the bank takes into account the balance in your savings account, offsetting that balance against your outstanding mortgage principal amount. As a result, your interest costs will be lower. Do read the fine print on any arrangement of this type, so you are clear about what cash balances will be taken into account, and if there are any constraints on how long you need to hold your cash in that bank for it to count for the offset.

- **Mortgage arrangement fee** – this is really important to consider when you think about your actual borrowing costs. It's the cost the mortgage provider charges you for setting up the mortgage, and is typically a fixed amount; this can be a pretty big number. You need to add this to your interest payments to figure out what the real cost of your borrowing will be, and you may be surprised at what a difference it makes to your APR. If you see a mortgage deal with a surprisingly low interest late, look at the arrangement fee. It is likely to be unusually high, and vice versa.

- **Early repayment/termination** – this is important to consider, not because you are thinking that you'll be able to repay your mortgage soon, but because you may want to change your mortgage deal as interest rates change. Many mortgage arrangements will have a relatively big lump-sum fee you'll have to pay to break the deal, so read this section of the mortgage agreement carefully before you sign. As an example, if you are on a fixed rate mortgage and rates fall significantly, you may want to change deals, but the cost of termination may make that prohibitive. And the cost of termination plus arrangement fee for a new mortgage may make it doubly so.

Utilities   Whether you rent or own a specific property, the utility costs will be the same, but utility costs can differ significantly by type of house. Charismatic old properties are frequently draughty and expensive to keep warm. New properties are usually environmentally friendly, which also means wallet friendly. Whether a place has electric, oil or gas heating, and the type of cooker and other white goods, will also impact utilities costs. A good starting point is to ask the estate agent about the prior owner's bills. You can also check out the environmental rating of a property online.

Council tax   This too is the same whether you own or rent the same property, but the amount will differ based on where you live. This is because the tax is the cost the local council is charging you for services it provides to you. Better services are more expensive. The annual tax should be disclosed on the estate agent's property particulars. Bear in mind that this figure can change year by year and the amount of change differs by council. You can pay the council tax in 10 monthly instalments rather than as a lump sum.

Ground rent/service charges   You'll see the word 'leasehold' or 'freehold' when you look at estate agents' property particulars. Put simply, if you buy a **freehold** property you own the land, and if it is a flat, you own part of the communal areas (eg hallway). If you buy a **leasehold** property, someone else owns the land and the communal areas. Either way, if you are buying a flat you'll need to figure in costs for your contribution to running the communal areas. In some cases, everyone in the building will pay a monthly or quarterly amount to build a fund ready for use when the roof needs redoing or the lobby needs repainting. In other cases, you'll be told to contribute as and when something needs doing. You need to ask about this so you are clear about what the financial demands on you may be. If the property is in a building of flats, the cost of insuring the whole building is likely to be included in the service charge. And if the building has any facilities like a gym, the cost of running that will also be included in the service charge.

Building insurance   When you rent a place, the building itself will be insured by the property owner and the cost will be factored into your rental payments. When you own your own place, you'll have to arrange your own building insurance – and it can be surprisingly expensive. If you buy a leasehold property, the cost may be included in the ground rent. But it's more likely that the ground rent includes only the overall building insurance and you'll need to arrange your own insurance for your part of the property (ie your flat). This insurance covers things like fixing the place if you have a fire, smoke or water damage, and fixing the flat below you if you have a leak that messes up their place.

Contents insurance   You will have insured yourself for loss (including theft) or damage to your stuff when you rented, which may have been for a substantial amount of stuff if your rental was unfurnished. Once you own a property, you'll probably have more stuff to insure. You'll need to estimate the total value of everything you own in order to get insurance quotes (remember curtains, clothes, equipment). It is a good idea to keep a folder of invoices (in a waterproof and fireproof cabinet) for any high-value things you buy, as it will make life easier if you ever have to file an insurance claim. It is also useful to review that file when your contents insurance comes up for renewal. And if you buy valuable things in between insurance renewal periods, let the insurer know immediately by phone, followed up by an e-mail or letter.

Upfront financial considerations   There are several financial things to consider when you are buying a property:

- **Property purchase price** – the biggest decision is how much money you want to spend, probably driven by how much you can borrow. The other constraint will be how large a deposit the lender requires. You may be able to pay that in cash from your savings, or you may borrow that money from other sources – but not from another bank, because your main bank won't allow that. The amount you spend will also be impacted by the anticipated running costs – the bigger the place, the higher the costs to run and furnish! And you'll also want to consider the cost of any repairs or planned refurbishments or decorating.

   o There are lots of ways to find properties, with estate agents nearly always involved in some way. Always remember that estate agents are working on behalf of the person *selling* the property and it is in their client's and their interests to get the highest price possible. When you're the buyer, they're not really concerned about you, though if they are really good they may make you feel as if they are. Agents are paid a fee by the seller – usually 1–3 per cent of the final price.

   o Once you start looking at properties, you'll get a good feel for pricing, as the market is very transparent. The area you look in will influence the price of a property. In London, Chelsea is more expensive than Elephant and Castle. In Manchester, Deansgate is more expensive than Fallowfield. And in Bristol, Clifton is more expensive than Hotwells. Once you start looking, you'll get a good idea of what a reasonable price for a specific property is.

o In general, properties in more desirable areas are easier to sell, and hold their value better, than those in less desirable areas. But they're usually more expensive to start out with as well. Some say it's all swings and roundabouts. What else to think about – how close is public transport, are there restaurants and shops nearby, and are there good schools in the area? In London, for example, property prices near Santander bike docking stations and areas near the new overground stations increased recently. Frequently, there are articles in newspapers, particularly the Sunday ones, about up-and-coming areas that can offer good value in terms of cost of purchase and a potential value appreciation.

- **Legal fees** – find a good lawyer, by checking with friends and family, to help guide you through the purchase process. The role your lawyer fulfils is critical, making sure you have good title to the property, checking to see if there is anything planned in the area that could impact the property price and quality of life there, eg a motorway being built on your doorstep. Lawyers will also handle the movement of monies and the necessary negotiations with the seller's lawyers. It's a good idea to ask the one you select what the likely cost of services will be, but in reality there are many factors that will have an impact on the cost. You don't want to worry about making social chit-chat with your lawyer, as they charge you by the minute. You do want to plan your meetings carefully in advance. You can ask for periodic, eg monthly or weekly, spending updates and bills, so you always know how much money you have spent.

- **Property surveyor fees** – you'll also need to find a property surveyor who will visit the property and inspect it closely. Surveyors are looking to see if there are any major repairs needed, and give an estimate of what they think the property is worth. You want them to find everything that's wrong, and the seller wants them to find nothing wrong! They'll provide a written report that lists what they have found and their view of the property's price.

o Armed with the report, you'll need to decide if you want to proceed with the purchase and if so, whether or not you're still happy with the price you originally agreed. If major work needs doing, you may want to negotiate the price down. Typical examples for which negotiation is likely include roof replacements, damp-related repairs and woodworm repairs. You want to know that for sure, as in some cases the seller can claim the cost of repairs on their insurance. You need to be fully informed before you finalize the deal by signing the papers.

o The surveyor will send their report to your lawyer and mortgage provider. There will be a problem if the surveyor's estimated value of the property is below the price you have agreed with the seller, because the lender may no longer be happy about lending you the full amount you wanted to borrow. This is because the lender wants to be absolutely sure that if you can't make your mortgage payments and they force you to sell the house, they will get the full amount of their loan back.

- **Stamp duty** – this is a tax imposed by the UK government on property purchases, paid by the property buyer. The tax charged is zero for a property valued up to £125,000; 2 per cent on the value between £125,001 and £250,000; 5 per cent on the value between £250,001 and £925,000; 10 per cent on the value between £925,001 and £1.5 million; and 12 per cent on the value in excess of £1.5 million. The government waives the stamp duty for first-time buyers on the first £300,000 of a property purchase, and £500,000 on a property being bought by more than one person. Check the HMRC website early in your planning, as the rates and waivers can change. Beginning in April 2015, the Scottish government introduced a Land and Buildings Transactions Tax; the details are available at www.revenue.scot/land-buildings-transaction-tax.

- **Estate agent fees** – When you sell a property, you will bear the cost of estate agent fees. New options are arising there too. It used to be you paid an agent 1–3 per cent of the selling price of your home; now purplebricks.co.uk and other firms are offering fixed-fee sales in the region of £900 or less.

Costs once you own a property The costs don't stop once you own the property. There are three types of purchases you'll need to make:

- **Furniture** – bear in mind that you don't have to fully furnish your home immediately – get the essentials and then go for incremental change. IKEA and eBay are good places to start; and think about second-hand purchases through websites like loot.com and preloved.co.uk. Look at freecycle.org for all sorts of free used things ranging from washing machines to shelving to furniture. If you work at it, you shouldn't have to pay full price for anything big. Wait for the mid-year sales for sofas, chairs, tables and negotiate at every shop, including the big retail chains. Look out for floor sample sales where you can really bargain on pricing, as the shop is trying to clear out what they have in stock to make room for new goods.

- **Appliances** – these can be quite costly. Hopefully the place you buy will come with what's essential. But essential is a funny term – all about expectations. Is a washing machine essential? How about a dishwasher? Tumble dryer? I will also include a vacuum cleaner in here, which you *do* need. When you make these biggish investments, you need to check out the warranty. A warranty guarantees that the provider will fix what you bought if it breaks, at no cost to you. The provider may also offer you an extended warranty, which requires you to pay an additional fixed amount up front to cover repair costs after the original warranty expires. In order to decide whether or not you take this, you have to do some maths. You need to consider the warranty cost versus the value of what you are buying. You could end up paying for the machine several times over in warranty costs. I'm not a big fan of extended warranties; I've read that retailers make more money from selling them than they make from the original sale of appliances. I find that, if I start with a good-quality piece of equipment and I take care of it, it tends to last well.

- **Garden equipment** – if you want a garden and can afford to have one, keep in mind that they cost money and time! You'll need to buy tools, plants, furniture and other things. You may find that having access to a communal garden or living near a park gives you what you need of the outdoors.

Armed with the information described above, you'll have what you need to do an easy analysis to help you make an overall buy-versus-rent decision. This will give you a general feel, but if you decide to buy, you'll want to do a detailed, property-specific analysis as you narrow down the properties you want to consider. It's definitely worth taking your time on the maths. And importantly, play around with the mortgage figure, as that's the one that can change dramatically owing to factors outside your control – changing interest rates.

And there you have it – the big money decisions you are likely to face and things to think about to help you make the most informed decisions and therefore the best decisions for you.

11
Getting and keeping a good credit score

A credit score, or credit rating, is an assessment of your creditworthiness; your ability to pay back any money that you borrow. That means an evaluation of how likely you are to meet your obligation to make interest payments and principal repayments.

Picture lending money to a friend. If you've lent them money before and they have repaid you, you are likely to lend them money again. If they haven't, or they've been late in paying and you've had to chase them up, you'll be hesitant about lending them money again. You are credit scoring your friend.

That is the same thing a bank or other lender does when you ask to borrow money. Those institutions need to decide how likely you are to pay back what you borrow. Unlike the situation with your friend, they don't know you; so they'll collect data from you and other sources in order to do their evaluation.

Who decides what your credit score/rating is?

Historically, many credit providers (eg banks, building societies, credit card and store card providers) did their own scoring. With the expansion of credit-rating agencies, lenders of all types are increasingly relying on information provided by those agencies to make their credit decisions. Credit-scoring agencies collect information about you from many sources, including credit cards, bankruptcy, court orders and so on – and from that, they derive a number that is classified as a good, mediocre or bad credit rating. A potential lender simply obtains your rating from the credit agencies' online system and, based on that, decides whether or not to lend you money.

That's why you want only *good* data about you available in the market – and why *you* need to check what is out there from time to time. To check your rating, you can look at Experian.co.uk, noddle.co.uk (this one is free of charge), www.creditexpert.co.uk/, www.totallymoney.com and www.equifax.co.uk.

How a financial picture of you is developed

As you move up the financial ladder, you create a credit picture for others to see. Here's a brief summary of how that happens.

Bank current account

You created your first personal financial record when you opened your first bank account. You create a new record each time you open a new bank account. Each time you open an account, you will have to prove that you are who you say you are. You'll be asked to provide a passport or driver's licence, and produce a bill or two that shows your current address. The bank will probably check that you're on the electoral register, and look to see if there is any bad financial information about you.

When a bank issues you with a debit card, as it is linked to your current account they won't perform additional checks as exposure to you is limited by the amount of cash in your account (plus an overdraft if you have one).

Bank overdrafts

When a bank offers you an overdraft, they are in effect agreeing to lend you money. An overdraft is like a safety net attached to your bank account. If your bank account balance goes below zero, cash will be provided from the overdraft facility. As mentioned in Chapter 7, some banks use this to attract new customers.

Managing any overdraft is important to your credit score. Taking one out is fine, but what matters hugely is how quickly you pay it back. So pay it back as soon as you can!

Credit cards

When your existing bank offers you a credit card, the process is likely to be fairly straightforward, as they know quite a bit about how financially responsible you are already. They have seen transactions in and out of your current and savings accounts, and can see if you have used any overdraft(s). On the credit card application form, you'll need to disclose any bank accounts, overdrafts, loans or other credit arrangements with other banks or with other credit providers.

Assuming your bank offers you a credit card, it will set a limit on the amount you can have outstanding on the card at any time. If, at a later date, you want to have that limit increased, the bank will review your financial records again to assess whether they think you can manage a bigger limit. I *cannot emphasize enough* how critical it is that you always pay at least the minimum monthly amount due on your credit card by the specified due date.

Other extensions of credit

When you apply for other credit cards or store cards, or buy goods on credit (like furniture), or take out smallish bank loans, the potential lenders will always follow the same basic process. You'll be asked to complete a questionnaire; the lender will take steps to validate the information you provide; and the lender will also check if you're on the electoral register. The lender will also check the credit score you have at one or a few of the credit agencies.

Home loan/mortgage

When you apply for a mortgage the lender is going to do a great deal of work before lending you money. (See Chapter 10 for more information.) At this stage, just understand that lenders will have specific criteria for you to meet in order to approve a mortgage, and this is where a good credit record is really important. The starting point for the amount of mortgage they offer will be a multiple of your base salary. Banks are very forthcoming about the multiple so that no one's time is wasted.

Once you figure out the bank you want to use, you'll have to go through a detailed application process, beginning with a questionnaire. They'll confirm your salary with your company; expect to be challenged *hard* by the bank to verify your earnings if you're self-employed. The point system banks use awards additional points for stability, including being with an employer for several years. They'll want to know all about your financial history, current position and future potential. All of this is aimed at assessing whether they feel comfortable that you will be able to make interest payments as they come due as well as pay back the principal. The UK regulator is putting additional pressure on banks to make sure they do enough work to satisfy themselves that the mortgage provided is affordable by the client, so expect even more questions and paperwork demands.

How credit scores are calculated

Credit scores are calculated based on answers to a pre-specified set of questions, including the following:

- Name – always use your legal name and include prior names if any have changed.
- Current address and how long you have lived there. If you have lived there less than three years, provide your previous address.
- Owner or renter at your current address?
- Are you on the electoral register? (You need to be.)
- Are you an employee or self-employed?
- What company do you work for? How long have you been working there? How long were you at your last employer?
- Provide a list of credit cards, the average balance, average monthly payments and credit limits.
- Provide debit card details.
- Provide details of any other indebtedness, including totals, monthly payments, and interest.
- Declare any county court judgments against you.

The credit agency/lender's point system will allocate points for each answer and the points will be added up to create a total score. This score will be turned into a yes or no for credit approval. If you have been working for the same company and living in the same house for 10 years, you are more likely to be given credit than if you have just moved to your house (and you move annually) and you haven't had a job for the past 10 years. They'll also consider how much credit/debt you have outstanding or could have outstanding.

This score is based on factual information provided by you in the first instance and then, depending on the amount of money involved, validated and/or supplemented by external information sources. For example, if you are buying furniture on credit, the company may well contact your bank to confirm information about your relationship with them. They may want to confirm your employment information. Or they may want to confirm the amount of rent you pay.

It may seem perverse, but to get a credit score, you need to show that you have borrowed money and paid it back. My best advice is that you get a credit card and use it, but never charge more on it than you can pay back in each month.

Keep it clean

When you think about it, it's obvious that you want a good credit score. However, it can be quite difficult to get one when you're coming out of education and starting your career, because you need a record of borrowing and paying back; and you'll probably have avoided borrowing. Even your phone contract may be in a parent's name (I suggest you get them to put it in your name from an early age even if they are paying for you), so you haven't created a credit history there. So be brave, get a credit card and use it, and pay off the full amount every month.

As you move around, make sure you don't leave unpaid bills, like electricity or gas, as they will damage your score. And keep the electoral register up to date.

Keep in mind that if you move to a new country, your credit-rating process starts from zero. Our son and daughter have both moved to New York City and faced this. Despite their great UK credit records, they had to pay six months' rent up front.

'Guard your credit rating by only applying for the right credit cards. In the past the only way you would know if you'd be accepted for a card was to apply. There are now handy tools like uSwitch.com's credit card checker to find out if you are likely to get approved. Getting rejected by credit card companies can damage your credit rating.'

Money Week

Your personal information

It may seem somewhat scary that people are collecting information about you and you don't know about it; sometimes the age of technology *doesn't* feel very comfortable. You can see your credit records using one of the services listed earlier. If your credit application is turned down, you have a right to ask the potential provider for an explanation of why you were rejected. It's possible that your application was turned down inappropriately; the lender may have received incorrect information.

You'll also want to check out some of your underlying data occasionally. I was shocked when my credit card application was rejected. When I investigated, I found that my home address was incorrect on Experian's records, so I didn't appear to be listed on the electoral register, the first test the lender applies. Easy enough to fix and I have done it, but what a lot of trouble due to the transposition of two words.

Your credit score – key points

In a nutshell, what you need to know:

- Anyone thinking about lending you money will do checks on you to evaluate how likely you are to meet your payment commitments.

- They will do the work themselves, or get data about you from other sources, like credit-scoring agencies.

- Keeping a good credit record is critical. It will give you financial options because people will be willing to lend you money. To keep your record clean, pay your bills on time and don't borrow more than you can afford.

- Getting a bad credit record *reduces* your financial options. You may find yourself unable to borrow money; be offered borrowings, but at very high interest rates to reflect perceived high risk; or only be able to borrow money from alternative sources, such as pawnbrokers and unauthorized money lenders. Getting a bad rating is easy – just don't pay your bills on time.

- Turning a bad credit score into a good one is hard work.

- Remember that other people can see your credit score. Remember that prospective employers have an established practice of performing credit checks.

- You can check out your credit score and underlying information for free on some webpages, so remember to do it from time to time.

12
Top money pitfalls to avoid

This chapter is a quick summary of the most common pitfalls of money management – the things that are most likely to derail you from your goal of being in control of your money. Keep this list in mind as an alarm list: pay extra attention to what you're deciding when you come across them.

> 'By adulthood, many UK citizens have not received a good enough financial education to ensure they can make the right choices and decisions when it comes to money matters.'
>
> Financial Inclusion Commission

Take your time when making a big money decision

When you're making a money decision, take the amount of money that is involved into account. If it's a small amount, you don't need to spend too much time thinking about it; just make sure it makes sense for you. The bigger the amount, the more time you want to take to think the decision through. If someone is rushing you into something, saying 'you'll miss this chance if you delay' – it's highly likely you should give it a miss.

Avoid the upward debt spiral

It is all too easy to get caught up in a cycle of taking on more debt. This is because once you are given some credit (like a credit card if you go to university), banks, credit card companies and other lenders seem to offer money all the time. I heard plenty of stories from people who had accepted credit and store cards when they were offered to them, and then ended up in a panic with debts they couldn't pay off. Pay attention to the information in the store cards and credit cards section of the book. If you really want the discount you get for the first use of a store card, use it, pay the amount off and get rid of the card. Use *one* credit card.

Sooner than you think, you'll be making decisions about how much money you allow yourself to borrow. How much money do you want to commit to renting a property? How big a mortgage will you be willing to take on to buy a home? How should you finance buying a new sofa? There will be lots of big decisions. What you decide for those and other situations will have been shaped by the money habits and values that you develop now and in the next few years.

Never mix short- and long-term debt

A big mistake that people make is paying off a long-term loan with a credit card. That will accelerate the deterioration of your financial situation; a long-term debt (eg mortgage) will have a long-term borrowing rate, which will always be lower than the short-term credit card interest rate. Put simply, if your mortgage interest rate is 4 per cent and your credit card interest rate is 19 per cent, it doesn't make sense to shift the debt to the higher-cost lender.

Pay attention to details

Read the small print on all financial commitments. That includes things like mobile phone contracts, property leases, and ordering stuff on the internet. Work through worst-case scenarios that could happen related to those decisions, such as: what if the value of the home you buy decreases by 50 per cent, what if you wreck the car, what if you lose your job, what if interest rates go up, what if interest rates go down?

Remain in control

Always remember that there are several groups who are always keen to get their hands on your money, so make it your job to remain in control when you deal with them. Let's take a quick run-through of what we have learned about who wants your money and what to look out for.

The tax authorities (HMRC)

The tax system is set up to assume that you work all year, so it's likely that when you work during summer and other breaks, and when you start your first permanent job, you will (at least initially) have more tax withheld than you owe. Pay close attention to every payslip – see Chapter 8 about payslips. If you think the tax withheld from your pay is incorrect, get in touch with your employer's tax office immediately. You'll need to have your National Insurance number handy. Make sure you make a note of who you have spoken with and follow up with a letter or e-mail to document the conversation.

The banks

- Once you have a current account with a bank, you need to be careful to avoid going overdrawn. Remember that anytime you tap to pay or use your debit card, the money comes out of your current account immediately.

- Think carefully about getting an overdraft. They are frequently offered to sixth-form and university students with a zero interest rate, which converts to a full interest rate at the end of education. Most banks will notify you before you use the overdraft, so you can take action to avoid using it.

- Reconcile your bank account regularly and check the balance every time you get money out of a cash machine.

- Manage the use of your debit card (like cash) and credit card closely.

- Shop around if you're looking for a loan for personal use, buying a car or buying a property. Your current bank is not necessarily going to give you the best deal – remember that loyalty doesn't pay.

Anyone you sign a contract with

Read any contract you're agreeing to *carefully*, and ask any questions you have. Pay attention to the term of the contract – how long is it; are you able to cancel it part-way through the contract term; what is the cost of early cancellation? A few specific examples:

- **Mobile phones** – figure out what you really need (that's different from want!) in terms of call minutes, texts and data usage. Review your last six months of itemized bills so that you negotiate based on call minutes and texts actually used, rather than what you think you've used. Be careful about making and receiving calls and text messages when you go outside the EU. Currently, EU law prohibits any roaming charges within the EU; however, what will happen after Brexit is unclear. If you're travelling outside the EU, you should have the option of paying for using your phone – this is worth considering so that you don't get charged for 'international' calls. I find the safest thing to do is to stick to Wi-Fi to reduce costs, and turn off data roaming as soon as I leave the UK. Use all types of communication to reduce your costs, like WhatsApp, Facetime and Skype. If you're going to be in another country for a while, consider getting a local pay-as-you-go SIM card.

- **Internet access** – this can involve big numbers, so make sure you fully understand the deal. A good friend of mine (who has earned lots of money in his career) was ranting about being ripped off for years by his internet deal at home; he was paying for something he didn't even need. It's hard to keep up with all the technology options and interconnected technology deals. Each time one technology-related contract is up for renewal, you should think about all of your technology contracts collectively.

- **Gyms** – if you sign up for a gym, make sure you *will* use it. Consider how often you realistically will use it, and figure out what the likely cost per visit will be. Consider the full range of gym types – government-supported, no-frills gyms or having a few pieces of equipment at home (easy to buy at deep discounts on the internet). Explore whether, if you teach a class or two, you can have free or discounted access.

Start saving early

Savings are crucial in building financial resilience. They help people meet unexpected demands, smooth peaks and troughs in income and spending and limit the need for borrowing. Yet only 41 per cent of UK citizens report having any savings. StepChange has estimated that having £1,000 of savings could have prevented half a million people from falling into problem debt.

Financial Inclusion Commission

It really is possible to save money, as set out in Chapter 6. A short-term goal is to have several hundred pounds on deposit for things that you might need. Figure out your target number based on what you think you could need – replacement tyres if you have a car, personal insurance, a special holiday. A nearish-term goal (you have to figure out the time it will take you, but I encourage you not to take too long) is to have enough cash savings to cover your necessary expenses for six months. Keep that money where you can get to it immediately, that is, not locked up for a period. You would be surprised at how many people in the UK have less than £100 in savings. You don't want to be in that position, as it's easy to head right into debt!

Manage a property you rent carefully

As you read in Chapter 10, there are plenty of potential pitfalls when you rent a property. Starting with the rental agent, get totally clear about what is and is not included in the rent and do your full sums before committing to the lease. Think about how, among the group sharing, you will handle the financial arrangements. Consider a house account that everyone pays into in advance of bills coming in and regular account top-ups by all flatmates. Moving in at the beginning of the lease and moving out are high money-risk moments. When you move in, do a full inventory – write lists of what is there, what marks are on the walls, and take pictures so no one can later question the state of the place when you moved in. And when you move out, do the same. Restore everything to the condition it was in when you arrived and make sure it is mega-clean.

Choose who you live with carefully

As we covered in the 'renting property' section of Chapter 10, think carefully about who you share with. Remember that it can be easier to live with people who *aren't* your close friends than those who are. This is even more important if you decide to buy a property jointly with someone else. I've heard quite a few stories about partners buying property together, followed by a break-up of the relationship and a nightmare process of unwinding the property deal. The same can be true of renting property.

If you need to borrow money for a short time, check your options carefully and make sure you will be able to pay it back

Chances are at some point you will have a short-term money need – if you do, think carefully about the options for borrowing (see Chapter 7). Short-term lenders (search under that and 'payday lenders' on the web) are now fewer in number than previously, owing to stricter regulation. They're likely to be your quickest route to cash. If you don't pay the money you borrow back on time, the penalties will be limited to 100 per cent of the amount you borrowed, but your credit rating will suffer.

Think before lending to, and borrowing money from, friends

In general, mixing friends and money is not a good idea. Even seemingly little amounts can go unpaid and strain a relationship, because the lender isn't quite sure how to ask for the money back. The only suggestion I can make is to write money borrowed or lent down as soon as the money changes hands. This even goes for the casual tenner when you're out and about. (It may be tough to write it down then and there, but make a point of the fact you are lending it and mention it the next day.) Someone said to me: 'If you can't afford for your friend not to pay back the money, don't lend it in the first place.' And if someone lets you down with repayments, don't keep lending to them. If you do borrow or lend a significant sum from or to a friend, do it on a commercial basis. That means giving/getting more interest than a bank would charge, so everyone wins.

Take steps to avoid identify theft and other crimes

The price of using technology in relation to money is that we're open to the risk of other people accessing our money through that technology. Criminals are always inventing new ways to get money through illegal means. You need to be super vigilant. A few ways to keep secure are:

- **Change your password** often and make it a complicated one. Always include at least one upper-case letter, one number and one special character, such as an exclamation mark or ampersand. The majority of criminals get in through poor passwords.

- **Never open a link** to your bank that is embedded in an e-mail. Never open an attachment to a bank's e-mail. And never open an e-mail from a bank you haven't done business with.

- **Always contact your bank** by going direct to the bank and not via other sources.

- **Consider getting a separate credit card** to use when buying things on the internet.

Historically, banks have automatically reimbursed customers for fraud, but many are beginning to reconsider this, instead putting pressure on customers to be more responsible for protecting themselves by adopting stronger passwords and increasing their vigilance concerning withdrawals.

Here are some pointers:

- **PIN codes** – *never* tell anyone else what your number is, and make sure no one sees the numbers you punch into any machine.

- **Credit cards** – in the UK we use chip and PIN, and the same warnings as above apply. But in other countries, where you may have to sign a credit card receipt, you will want to keep a copy of the receipt you sign. In some countries, your card may be run through a funny machine that has carbon paper in it. If so, you want your receipt copy and the carbon paper.

- **Cashless payments** – payments can now be made in lots of different ways: tapping a debit card (up to a limited amount), tapping a credit card, tapping your travel card, tapping your phone and who knows what next? Two important risks are emerging with these. First is 'card clash', where two of your cards get charged for the same thing. Think Oyster and debit card as you go through an underground barrier or get on a bus. Keep your cards separate and only put one next to the reader. Second is when a thief passes their card reader by your card and 'collects' money from you. I have heard of this happening at crowded tube stations where the thief quickly collects thousands of pounds. This makes it increasingly important that you check your bank account frequently and make sure you investigate any irregularities as soon as you see them!

- **Cash machines** – these also pose risks. It's best to use machines that are located inside or outside a bank branch. If you notice anything at all unusual about the machine as you are using it, immediately cancel the transaction and get your card back. If the machine swallows your card for no apparent reason, report it immediately. Don't let anyone look over your shoulder as you are using the machine, even if they are trying to be helpful in some way.

- **Avoid wallet/handbag theft** – this of course isn't totally under your control, but you can take a few precautions (and don't think this is just women!). Make sure your bag can be closed properly and make sure your wallet is at the bottom of the bag. When you're in crowds, including tubes and buses, keep your bag closed (my wallet was stolen from my unzipped handbag on a crowded tube); or, keep your wallet in your front jacket or trouser pocket. Backpacks are great, but it's easy for someone to slit the bottom and take what they want, so keep it in front of you when you're in a crowd. It's a big mistake to leave a handbag, backpack, laptop or anything else on the back of a chair, on the floor, on the table in a restaurant or any other public place, as it's *very* easy for someone to steal it. (I know more than a handful of friends this has happened to.) If it does happen, call your debit and credit card companies immediately. They'll ask you what the numbers of your cards are – how are you supposed to know that if the card has been stolen? – so keep a list of the cards you have, the card numbers and contact information stored somewhere, in case you need it. Somewhere separate from your bag and wallet, of course. The information is also on the credit card statements – another good reason to keep them around.

- **Avoid getting mugged** – this clearly has implications beyond money and technology, but this seemed like the best place to include it. Keep these things in mind:

  o Trust your instincts. If you're uncomfortable about someone sitting next to you, walking near you or something else, do something about it. Don't worry about causing offence or being embarrassed.

  o Stay away from deserted areas and be extra vigilant in large crowds.

  o Be aware at all times. This means not walking down the street listening to music, talking on your mobile phone or texting/e-mailing. Step out of the stream of people traffic and stop walking to do anything on your phone; you'll see people doing these things all the time, totally oblivious to their surroundings, which puts them at risk – I've seen some potentially fatal near-misses with cars and buses and people. Avoid this risk to yourself.

o If you're mugged, give the person what they want. You can even throw your bag, wallet, phone, computer or whatever it is the mugger wants aside, so the mugger goes after that and not you. This is not the time to think about anything other than your personal safety.

- **Get to know your debit and credit card helplines** – the more your debit/ credit card company knows about you, the more it can do to protect you. Ring to tell the company if you're travelling, to ensure you won't get stuck being unable to use your card in some distant place as they think your card has been stolen.

- **Respond quickly** to calls from your credit card company's fraud department – these calls are initiated because, for some reason, their data-mining work has indicated that someone may be using your card fraudulently. You'll need to respond to a series of questions about recent purchases. To make it easy for the company to find you, make sure your contact details held by them are kept up to date. Don't be alarmed if a vendor gets an instruction to ring the card company when you go to use a card, as the company may be just checking for fraud reasons.

- **Protect your information** – whenever possible, put security codes on your laptop, tablet, mobile phone and any other equipment. By doing so, if you do lose it, at least the information won't be available to whoever has it to cause damage by incurring costs. Avoid using open WiFi accounts at all times – they leave you exposed to other people easily accessing your information.

- **Back up your data regularly** – always back up your data, including the data on your laptop and phone. You'll need to set this up on your devices. If you have an Apple phone, your data will automatically be backed up for you, as long as you are connected to WiFi and you're within your storage allowance.

- **Clean up your computer** when you're finished with it – before giving your computer to a charity or disposing of it in another way, delete all of the information stored within it.

And some good news

There's plenty of support to help you make informed money decisions all the time. Resources include:

- The internet is a great source of information on all things money related. Relevant websites were mentioned throughout the book, and new ones will continue to emerge. Do make sure you're aware as to whether a given site is independent or not. There are also an increasing number of blogs and videos which can be found by carrying out a general internet search.

- Newspapers also are good sources of information on money issues. The money sections of the Sunday papers are useful, as they include topical pieces. Newspapers also provide information about the political, social and financial environment, all of which will impact you and your money.

- Travel plans are best made early using comparison websites such as expedia.co.uk and kayak.co.uk. And the very confusing train travel pricing is best conquered via the internet, as no one could possibly be on top of an explanation of all the available options. One of the easiest ways to stretch your cash is to plan ahead. Of course, that is easier said than done!

- Fashion can be a cheap product now, with shops like Primark, and lots of discount shopping available on the internet. But if you want to buy quality pieces at a discount, wait for the major summer sales at the main shops or specialist high-quality internet sites like net-a-porter.com and outnet.com. There are new ones springing up all the time.

- Using coupons is a great way to save money – vouchercloud, Groupon and myvouchercode are all accessible via smartphones or the internet. You can also take advantage of paper-based offers, and make sure you use loyalty points awarded in stores, on airlines, and all sorts of other places. Sometimes I feel like a real dope when I pay full price for something!

INDEX